Waging Cyber War

Technical Challenges and Operational Constraints

Jacob G. Oakley

Apress®

Waging Cyber War: Technical Challenges and Operational Constraints

Jacob G. Oakley
Owens Cross Roads, AL, USA

ISBN-13 (pbk): 978-1-4842-4949-9   ISBN-13 (electronic): 978-1-4842-4950-5
https://doi.org/10.1007/978-1-4842-4950-5

Managing Director, Apress Media LLC: Welmoed Spahr
Acquisitions Editor: Susan McDermott
Development Editor: Laura Berendson
Coordinating Editor: Rita Fernando

Cover designed by eStudioCalamar

Distributed to the book trade worldwide by Springer Science+Business Media New York, 233 Spring Street, 6th Floor, New York, NY 10013. Phone 1-800-SPRINGER, fax (201) 348-4505, e-mail orders-ny@springer-sbm.com, or visit www.springeronline.com. Apress Media, LLC is a California LLC and the sole member (owner) is Springer Science + Business Media Finance Inc (SSBM Finance Inc). SSBM Finance Inc is a **Delaware** corporation.

For information on translations, please e-mail rights@apress.com, or visit http://www.apress.com/rights-permissions.

Apress titles may be purchased in bulk for academic, corporate, or promotional use. eBook versions and licenses are also available for most titles. For more information, reference our Print and eBook Bulk Sales web page at http://www.apress.com/bulk-sales.

Any source code or other supplementary material referenced by the author in this book is available to readers on GitHub via the book's product page, located at www.apress.com/9781484249499. For more detailed information, please visit http://www.apress.com/source-code.

Printed on acid-free paper

To my children, you'll move mountains.

Table of Contents

About the Author

Dr. Jacob G. Oakley spent over 7 years in the US Marines and was one of the founding members of the operational arm of Marine Corps Forces Cyberspace Command, leaving that unit as the senior Marine Corps operator and a technical lead. After his enlistment, he wrote and taught an advanced computer operations course, eventually returning back to mission support. He later left government contracting to do threat emulation and red teaming at a private company for commercial clients, serving as principal penetration tester and director of penetration testing and cyber operations. He is working as a cyber SME for a government customer. He completed his doctorate in IT at Towson University researching and developing offensive cyber security methods. He is the author of the book *Professional Red Teaming* (Apress, 2019) and the technical reviewer of the book *Cyber Operations, Second Edition* (Apress, 2019), by Mike O'Leary.

About the Technical Reviewer

Wayne York is a retired Marine with over 20 years of service and experience ranging from systems administration, digital network analysis, signals intelligence, and cyber operations. He was involved in the stand-up of the Marine Corps Forces Cyberspace Command with nearly a decade spent between the headquarters and operational components. His time in the Marines as a warfighter and cyber operations subject matter expert provides insight into the complexities of the cyberspace domain.

He is now a senior penetration tester with a professional services company and works both commercial and government contracts helping ensure customers secure their networks and applications from adversarial cyber threats. He holds a Bachelor of Science in Computer Networks and Cybersecurity from the University of Maryland University College, as well as Security and Certified Ethical Hacker (CEH) certifications.

Acknowledgments

I thank my beautiful wife and family for sacrificing their nights and weekends to let me write this book and for loving and supporting me through this and other nerdy endeavors.

I thank my father for exemplifying hard work and for all he did to give me the best chance to succeed in life.

I would like to thank Wayne York for being the technical reviewer for this book and being a true leader of Marines, specifically this Marine.

To all you keyboard-wielding cyber warriors out there protecting freedom, I salute you.

Introduction

This book was written to inform the reader on the increasingly intertwined concepts of war and cyber. It is meant to dispel the misconceptions and mythos surrounding cyber warfare. Reading this book will provide insight into the technical obstacles within the cyber domain which hinder effective warfighting operations. You will also come to understand how legal and oversight authorities, as well as international convention, further constrain what technical capabilities do exist. Cyber warfare has crept into facets of everyday life. Each individual citizen and their personal devices, from cell phone to smart fridge, represent an extension of a nation's attack surface. Whether you are a policy maker, commander, warfighter, technical or non-technical citizen, or employed in the cyber security industry, understanding the facts of cyber warfare is necessary to combat its increasing pervasiveness.

CHAPTER 1

Cyber and Warfare

There is an awful lot of hype and confusion surrounding the concept of cyber warfare. It is certainly a term that has gained traction recently in the media and in military and government discussions. As ambiguous as the term cyber is itself, cyber warfare seems to suffer from even more variance and mischaracterization in its definition, doctrine, and implementation. Fortunately, I believe that in understanding warfare and cyber separately we can societally come to a more standardized and widespread acceptance of what it means to defend ourselves in a cyber war, conduct cyber warfare, and perhaps globally define what is and is not acceptable in such conflicts.

To properly understand what it will mean to go to war through cyber means we must unilaterally understand and cede to the truth and challenges that would exist in such combat. We cannot continue to apply known paradigms to a novel concept. "The Charge of the Light Brigade" is regaling and heroic; however, it was decimating and futile, and casualties were excessive. If we keep trying to think of cyber warfare as simply shooting like-sized cyber bullets at our enemy for similar or more improved effect or applying monolithic military doctrine without a technical understanding to cyber warfare, we will fail. Educating people, policy makers, and warfighters has to start somewhere, and I hope that in providing the ground truth of the technical and tactical challenges to waging a cyber war, we can together approach the future of warfare more informed.

Definition

First and foremost, what must be accepted is that war has not changed with the advent of the cyber buzzword. Cyber is just another way to carry out war, just like trench warfare, nuclear warfare, and any of the other categories of warfighting established throughout history. The United States Department of Defense (DoD) established its Cyber Command on October 31, 2010. From its homepage you can read its mission which is "to direct, synchronize, and coordinate cyberspace planning and operations to

© Jacob G. Oakley 2019
J. G. Oakley, *Waging Cyber War*, https://doi.org/10.1007/978-1-4842-4950-5_1

defend and advance national interests in collaboration with domestic and international partners."[1] Now, that does not sound particularly like warfighting, but on August 27, 2017, President Donald Trump decided to elevate USCYBERCOM from a sub-unified command to a Unified Combatant Command responsible for cyberspace operations. Also, from the USCYBERCOM web site, "The decision to elevate USCYBERCOM was seen as recognition of the growing centrality of cyberspace to U.S. national security and an acknowledgment of the changing nature of warfare."

These statements and declarations need some further clarification to really understand where we are going with these concepts. First starters, what is cyberspace? Merriam-Webster defines it as "the online world of computer networks and especially the Internet." The DoD recognized cyberspace as a warfighting domain, which means it is considered to be as encompassing as air, land, sea, or space, which are the other warfighting domains. This means that computer networks are to be viewed as the space within which we can maneuver, attack, and defend just like we do in warfare conducted in the other domains. Merriam-Webster defines war primarily as "a state of usually open and declared armed hostile conflict between states or nations" and warfare as "military operations between enemies." So, a deductive definition of cyber warfare is military operations carried out over computer networks in a declared conflict between state or nation enemies. This may seem like an oversimplification; however, it is the foundation for understanding the challenges of carrying out such military operations.

Declaration

With the workings of a definition for cyber warfare established, we next need to focus on the action that officially initiates war in general, cyber or otherwise, which is a declaration of war. This is an important topic to cyber-specific warfare for many reasons. Regardless of the domain a war is fought in if war is declared by a state; there are ethical, legal, and other implications that now apply to all following actions.

A state goes to war by declaring war in response to an act of war. That is essentially how an acknowledged armed conflict between states would begin. This is quintessentially illustrated by the bombing of Pearl Harbor by the Japanese during World War II. There was an act of war by the Japanese in using uniformed military actors to perpetrate a state-acknowledged act of aggression on US uniformed military actors

---

[1]www.cybercom.mil/About/Mission-and-Vision/

against targets in US sovereign waters and airspace and on US soil. In response to this, the US Congress, as the body with authority to do so, declared war against the Empire of Japan. The power to declare war is given to the US Congress in article one section eight of the US constitution. For perspective, the United States has only declared war 11 times, beginning with Great Britain in the war of 1812 and last with 6 individual declarations against specific countries during World War II.

It is an interesting thought experiment to ponder what type of cyber act it would take to convince the United States to declare war. Unlike conventional war, an act of war that was solely within the realm of the cyber domain is difficult to conceive. Slightly more analogous might be a cyber-enabled effect, where the cyber domain is used to control or effect some physical asset that might have widespread mortal effects worthy of a declaration war. Even this is extremely challenging as adequately attributing such an action to a state without an admission from that state is nearly impossible, we will cover more on that later. At this point we can essentially make two summations regarding cyber and warfare.

First, a cyber act of war almost assuredly will involve a cyber-physical connection and not simply stay within the realm of cyber. For instance, an attack fully within the cyber domain using a virus which cripples computers across all air force air bases is highly impactful to our national defense, but not likely to draw the US Congress into declaring war against the perpetrator. On the other hand, an attack that uses a computer virus to simultaneously take over the computers on nearly 100 air force aircraft involved in a large annual exercise and crash them all into the desert, killing nearly 1000 uniformed soldiers might be enough to result in a declaration of war against the perpetrator.

Second, with the exceedingly difficult obstacles to reliable attribution of cyber actions, the perpetrator of a cyber act of war would almost have to do so with the intent of acknowledging that action and starting a war. Even in the huge aggression of the cyber-physical example where billions of dollars in damages, thousands of deaths happen in a US sovereign area, if no perpetrator admits to the attack, what requirements must there be on an attribution to convince Congress to declare war on what they think to be the perpetrator. We will cover attribution in several chapters later in this book, but even at this juncture, trying to discern the type of proof Congress would require to declare war seems a daunting, if not impossible, task.

Even with the establishment of cyber warfare, it is only one of many warfighting domains, and Congress would have to be comfortable enough in the impact and identification involved in a cyber act of war to respond with armed conflict in all warfighting domains. As entertaining as the idea may be, I don't think the United States is going to respond to malicious email solicitation by a Nigerian Prince by sending aircraft and naval vessels and deploying troops to Nigeria after performing intercontinental missile strikes on their military bases. The ridiculousness of this example is easy to see, coming up with what credible cyber act deserves such a response is nowhere near trivial.

Just War Theory

Just war theory is essentially a set of requirements that must be met for a war to be considered just. It focuses on two essential criteria, the right to go to war and the right to conduct within a war. This is a largely philosophical concept but one that international law with regard to war often mirrors, references, or mimics. Further, policies and guidelines such as international law and just war theory place constraints on warfare and the warfighter such that they need to be understood before we explore how such policy-level restrictions manifest themselves as technical challenges in war and especially cyber warfare in later chapters.

Jus ad Bellum

The concept of the justice of war involves war being waged while respecting several constructs. There is having a cause that is just, for example, self-defense or defense of an ally. War must be conducted as a last resort to efforts such as diplomacy. A state going to war must do so with the appropriate authority, which in the case of the United States is with a declaration by Congress. The intent to go to war must be just and not self-serving, for instance, the annexation of Crimea could by some be viewed as self-serving and unjust, though, philosophically speaking, many Russians presumably view the activity as just or choose to not acknowledge as a state action of war. A war should only be started with a reasonable chance at success and be proportionate to the way it is waged.

A lot of this concept is strongly philosophical and too subject to debate to be involved in the discussions of technical obstacles in cyber warfare. That being said, several do lend themselves well to influencing and shaping actions during war in the domain of cyber. For instance, being conducted under the proper authority is an easily provable and understood concept as we have specific constitutional references that dictate how war may be declared. We also have various titles of the US Code which dictate that activity such as cyber warfare must happen under appropriate authorities itself. Intention can certainly be framed in cyber, specifically as it is in wider warfare. For instance, using cyber warfare to steal money from banks of other states for the sole purpose of profit would certainly be understood to be with unjust intentions. A war should only be declared with a reasonable chance of success, and I believe that construct should aptly apply to the technical aspects of cyber warfare. For example, launching a computer worm which spreads from computer to computer that will destroy all the data on that computer but which has only a 2% chance of targeting the machines whose data you need destroyed might be viewed as having little chance of success. Avoiding the use of cyber warfare in such situations certainly keeps the activity more on the side of just than not based on the likelihood of success and prevents those uninvolved in the conflict from facing its affects.

Jus in Bello

The concept of just actions while at war is based on the two principles of discrimination and proportionality. Essentially the reason for differentiating between *jus ad bellum*, the justice of going to war, and *jus in bello*, justice while conducting warfare, is to diverge the cause of the conflict from the actions within it. It may, for instance, be viewed as just for the United States to declare war against the Empire of Japan after Pearl Harbor. Conversely, actions during that war, for instance, the nuclear bombings of Hiroshima and Nagasaki, are polarizing actions viewed by some as just and by others as unjust.

Using the nuclear bombing example, let's explore the event while looking at it through the lens of jus in bello—was it a just or unjust action while being within a just war? Using the concept of discrimination, it would seem that the action was almost certainly unjust. Any offensive action must be carried out in a way that discriminates between combatants and innocents. The bombings certainly could not and did not do this, and many innocent lives were lost in both bombings. When looked at from the second perspective of just warfare, that actions should be proportionate to the desired objective, it becomes a much fuzzier decision.

Though indiscriminate, the proportion of deaths caused by the bombings compared to the deaths that would have happened on both sides during the rest of the island warfare being carried out on Japan and nearby areas favors the bombings and resulting surrenders. This is likely true of both combatant and non-combatant deaths on the side of the Japanese and certainly for combatants on the allied side. Through this lens it may be viewed as a just action within a just war, and certainly the decision makers who opted for the bombing must have felt so.

Just warfare has a large impact on the way cyber warfare should be carried out. Discrimination is extremely important given the interconnected nature of the cyber warfighting domain. We must ensure that if we carry out cyber warfare, we are able to have our offensive actions discriminate between combatants and non-combatants and even between targets within the declared enemy state and those without. In other warfighting domains such as air, land, and sea, it is not very likely that we accidently invade an ally, an abstainer, or even perhaps our own country.

Within the domain of cyber however, it can be extremely challenging to limit targeting to a specific enemy state while avoiding the occurrence of the effect acting upon a non-combatant or even a different nation state's asset. Let's take, for example, the Stuxnet virus, which almost certainly targeted the country of Iran and is largely heralded as an act of cyber warfare. Even in this advanced and very specifically targeted malware deployment, infections happened across the globe in many countries and in varying amounts. Certainly, all of the countries infected were not the target, and some were likely even allies to those which deployed the virus.

Proportionality is an extremely challenging constraint on cyber warfare as well. Take, for example, a cyber warfare offensive action that will shut down the power to the cyber-attack assets of another country. That in itself is certainly viewable as a just action of cyber warfare. But what if that same virus coincidentally also shut down the power to all the hospitals, traffic control systems, and water treatment plants of the target state. The objective of this action was to turn off the power to the cyber-attack assets of the enemy state; however, the result of the action would be considered in no way proportionate to that goal and would then be unjust. Once a cyber-attack has been launched, it can oftentimes be nearly impossible to cancel or reign back in and retarget completely. If the computers were shut down, it certainly can't be reversed or undone.

Many of the technical challenges discussed later in this book will hinge on these concepts to show how they impact war in general. Any state should strive in conducting cyber warfare to be as discriminate and proportionate as possible with the targeting of the offensive effects. When carried out successfully, such effects are a part of just warfare in a just war as illustrated in Figure 1-1. This must be done within the war such that the war can be declared justly and the actions within it, whether in the domain of cyber, land, air, space, or sea, can still be considered just themselves.

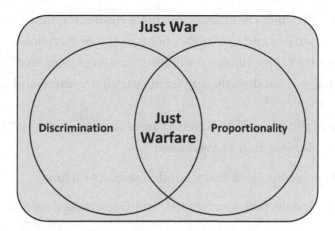

Figure 1-1. *Just Warfare in a Just War*

International Agreements

Even in a just war, wherein just actions are continuingly taking place, the fog of war and its general ugliness negatively impact all those involved and, in many cases, even those not involved. With a proper and legal declaration as well as staying within the philosophical bounds of just war and just warfare, there is still a need to further protect humans from the unfortunate byproducts of conflict. Though there are several active agreements and many historical ones, the most well known and oft applied is the Geneva Convention. The Geneva Convention and international agreements like it, such as the Hague Convention and others, all constitute what is known as international humanitarian law. These laws mainly aim to regulate warfare with respect to respecting the rights of the individual people who never, or no longer are able to, participate in armed conflicts between states. Those who were never involved may be abstainers or civilians or medical and religious personnel within involved states or simply members of nearby states who were participating in the conflict. Those no longer able typically consist of the injured, prisoners of war, or surrendered forces.

The Geneva Convention also outlines the obligations of other states, both involved and not involved, to uphold the agreed-upon standards. The onus here being on both participating and by-standing states in armed conflict being able to hold accountable individuals or states which violate the Geneva and Hague Conventions. Such violations constitute war crimes under international law and are often tried by an international tribunal at the Hague. Examples of this being many World War II German generals and government officials as well as modern-day issues like shootings by Blackwater contractors in Iraq and actions in Russia-Chechnya conflicts. It may be difficult to conceptualize cyber warfare and war crimes being tied together; however, as we explore the facets of the Geneva Convention, we will see that a large portion of the agreements are at least tangentially, if not directly, applicable to cyber warfare and its resulting effects.

Modernization of the initial 1895 Geneva Convention began in 1949 after World War II and included the following four conventions:

- The first two protect sick and wounded soldiers on land.

- The second protects sick, wounded, and shipwrecked soldiers at sea.

- The third protects prisoners of war.

- The fourth protects civilians, including those in occupied territory.

It is hard to imagine in today's world and the near future that the first three conventions would be much of a guiding force for anything related to cyber warfare or other activities in the cyber domain. It does not take much extrapolation though to see that the first two, protecting the sick and wounded, can apply to attacks that may affect those individuals indirectly. Examples of such cyber-attacks could be the purposeful targeting of devices within and resources of places such as hospitals. Both field and traditional civilian hospitals house and care for individuals protected by the first two conventions, and any cyber-attack that hampers the ability of those individuals to receive care could certainly be perceived as a violation of the Geneva Convention. The least applicable of the original four conventions is seemingly the third, related to prisoners of war. Though there are certainly cyber-attacks that could negatively impact the standard of living of prisoners of war, the affected facilities and faculties responsible for managing and caring for prisoners of war would likely belong to the same country launching such a cyber-attack. It thus seems currently unlikely that a cyber-attack would infringe upon the third Geneva Convention specifically regarding prisoners of war.

The fourth convention has very interesting applications to current-day warfare and cyber warfare specifically. This convention protects civilians in general and calls out protection for those civilians in an enemy state-occupied area. Typically, this would seem to apply to persons like those French populations in German-occupied areas of France during World War II. A war including warfighting activities in a cyber domain puts an interesting twist on this, and the implications of different interpretations of this international law have yet to be fully explored with regard to cyber warfare.

Does a civilian's computer or cell phone reside within the bubble of protection afforded to civilians in wars under the Geneva Conventions? Is it thus a war crime under international law to use an unwitting civilian's laptop, smart fridge, or cell phone to redirect state cyber-attacks in an effort to avoid attribution of the attacker location? Similarly, is it a war crime to use an unwitting and innocent bystander's cell phone and its Wi-Fi communication ability to spread viruses into an enemy state's military installation network? As we will discuss in later chapters, attribution is extremely challenging, but in the cases where it happens, it is worth considering if we risk war crime implications by such actions.

This is important for the uniformed individual and the state involved. It also complicates the burden put upon signatories of the Geneva Convention to hold responsible those who commit what is understood to be war crimes. Can we really expect multiple uninvolved states to bring to military tribunal actors in a cyber war for such seemingly benign actions? Should we? These are heavily philosophical thoughts whose answers are best left for other people (probably lawyers?) and other literature (probably court proceedings), but at some point, the prevailing expectation of privacy in the cyber domain will lead to legal challenges to such behavior by states in the international law forum.

Other protocols amended to the Geneva Convention expand the document from one which pertains to state conflicts on an international stage to one that handles non-international conflicts by non-state-sponsored actors and everything in between. Further it has been refined to address types of weaponry and warfare that are deemed illegal or whose use is governed by international law. Such items include everything from cluster mines, chemical warfare to lasers, and other technologies. Interestingly enough the Geneva Convention has yet to have any language describing proper or improper use of cyber warfare and cyber weapons. Granted, as we have just discussed, the conventions still widely apply to war in general including efforts via the cyber domain, but perhaps it is a worthwhile pursuit to get the signatory states on board with at least some overarching dictation regarding how cyber warfare should or at least specifically how it should not be conducted to protect humanitarian rights on all sides. In the later chapters of this book, we will cover analogous examples on how and why cyber warfare and the cyber warfighting domain could be handled by international law. These same analogies, once properly understood, also allow for warfighters and policy makers to know why cyber warfare doesn't necessarily afford the actions and impacts many attribute to it.

Expectation of Protection

Considering the expected conduct of appropriately going to war and the humanitarian protections that go into it is extremely important regardless of the mediums the warfighting happens across. Another aspect of warfighting that is not fully appreciated in the auspice of cyber warfare is the fact of expected protection. Traditionally this is a concept that is little discussed and generally assumed as a given for warfighting. In the most basic sense, take, for example, the deployment of troops to a foreign nation. Regardless of the reason for that deployment, the citizens of the United States have an expectation that if we are deploying uniformed military personnel to another nation that we are also capable of preventing like repercussions here at home.

If Congress declared war against Japan in World War II when we as a nation were incapable of keeping uniformed Japanese soldiers from landing and taking over portions of this country, the populace would likely not support the war. This example is rather extreme, but even in modern terms, the nation largely understands that part of the reason we are deploying troops to embattled Middle Eastern nations is to keep the fighting there and not within the United States or its territories. This is the same for many countries and conflicts throughout the ages. Indeed, a huge factor behind a healthy fighting force which prevents absences without leave (AWOL) or mutiny is that the members of that fighting force have an expectation that while they are away fighting their nation's battles, their family is protected at home.

The underlying structure for the expectation of protection is that of boundaries. There is a benefit to being in countries such as the United States in that, while within the borders, national waters or airspace of the country, you can expect to be protected from the warfighting actions of others. This means that while you are in the United States, as a citizen or a visitor, you feel reasonably protected that, though the United States may be launching Tomahawk missiles at Syrian military bases under the direction of the Commander in Chief, there will not be a response in kind. Or, that when the United States similarly violates the sovereign airspace of Pakistan to capture or kill Osama bin Laden that other nation state helicopters won't be landing in your back yard any time soon. It also means that while Iran claims the United States is violating its national waters by sailing through the straits of Hormuz, you don't have to be worried about your chartered fishing boat being boarded or sunk by Iranian naval vessels while off the coast of Florida.

This situation is understood to be true both of conflicts a nation's forces are involved in, such as those just discussed but also simply as a resident of a nation. Even, perhaps especially, when a nation is not involved militarily in international affairs, there is an expectation that while within that nation's border, waters, and airspace, you have protections from outside malicious efforts, state-sponsored warfighting or otherwise.

Applying this to the cyber domain is extremely complicated. While browsing the internet from a device physically located in the United States, you may, for instance, travel through routing devices in many countries before you are presented with the web page of the web address you entered into your browser. Do you expect that the United States will protect you from downloading a virus that is part of a nation state's cyber warfare efforts? Could you? The answer is no; that would be ridiculous. The reason it is ridiculous is that by nature and intention most of the internet is essentially borderless. You don't have to provide a digital passport when your browsing habits take you to web sites hosted by servers outside the United States.

What is rather ironic is that most of the population of this country and others have this profound belief that the internet should be free of regulation and restriction while also being furious that their government was helpless to stop this international meddling attack or that state-sponsored cyber effort. It shouldn't really be that surprising that without a national cyberspace, there can't really be a realistic expectation of protection. This may seem preposterous, but I believe that if cyber-attacks and cyber warfare got bad enough, we will actually see more countries going the way of China and North Korea where there is a hard delimiter between where the nation's infrastructure and regulations apply and there they don't.

I am not suggesting countries adopt the suppressive behavior of these nations, but I do think that to protect the home front, we have to have a home front. Try and think of everything you own that has an ability to be somehow networked to the internet. Smart things and the internet of things are driving the potential attack surface of even a single individual to inconceivable breadth. The challenge of securing the digital attack surface of every citizen in this country from external cyber activity of nation states and other actors is insurmountable if we do not establish a boundary wherein we consider actions punishable under US law and are able to defend it as known US cyberspace. Further, if citizens do not know when they have left US cyberspace, they do not know when they are giving up their nation given protections in the cyber warfighting domain. An even more unique thought in that vein, is there some level of activity where even when out of US cyberspace, are you still expected to be protected from other state actors? Should alliances and treaties stretch into and be upheld in cyber as well? When I travel to another country, particularly an ally of the United States, I feel relatively safe due in no small part to my US citizenship. Currently in cyber and on the internet, this is essentially non-existent but perhaps that should evolve.

I say this not to put forward that I am a huge advocate of closing borders on the internet. I will admit that it is the most efficient way I can think of toward establishment of a national cyberspace and a resulting expectation of protection. I think the point of expected protection from the warfighting capabilities of other nations, including cyber warfare, is extremely salient and that this book would be incomplete without illustrating why this is so challenging defensively.

Summary

This chapter was intended to provide an initial overarching understanding of what is meant by the terms cyber warfare and the cyber domain of war. We also covered what it means to declare war and some of the pursuant activities. The theory of just war was discussed to provide some details on the philosophical constraints to any attempt at warfighting, with examples of cyber activity in such guidelines. International law and its involvement and effect on cyber warfare was outlined as was the difficulty in establishing an expectation of protection from cyber warfare activities.

CHAPTER 2

Legal Authority

Title 10 and Title 50 of the US Code are legal documents that outline the responsibilities of the Department of Defense (DoD) and Intelligence Community (IC), respectively. These two documents—with regard to war itself and cyber warfare specifically—are often poorly understood, misrepresented, and incorrectly cited. The intense interest and scrutiny in these documents is related to the legal authority they endow and the manner and responsibility for oversight of actions within that authority. I will do my best to efficiently summarize the importance of these documents to the warfighter and to cyber warfare itself as well as covering a third type of activity in covert action. I will also attempt to establish a fairly reliable line where activity must be done in the constraints of one title or another. I will further discuss examples of how this affects technical aspects of cyber warfare.

Title 50—Intelligence Community

For the sake of easier explanation and understanding of examples later, I will discuss Title 50 first. As was mentioned earlier, Title 50 outlines roles and responsibilities and authorities for the Intelligence Community. Title 50 is actually labeled as "War and National Defense" and has many chapters within it covering many topics. These chapters are as varied as espionage, the Central Intelligence Agency (CIA), and the National Security Agency (NSA), to those dealing with Merchant Ship Sales, Helium, Absentee Voting, and Wind Tunnels. For the purposes of this book though, we will focus on its direction and authority to the Intelligence Community for its activities under Title 50 and the Intelligence Committee oversight of those activities. In fact, much of the focus on discerning the difference between Title 50 and Title 10 actions is due to Intelligence Committees insisting it has oversight on the correct application of authority, actions within that authority, and budgetary oversight over Title 50 actions and often misunderstanding or perhaps purposefully attempting to paint Title 10 activities as falling under their Title 50 purview.

© Jacob G. Oakley 2019
J. G. Oakley, *Waging Cyber War*, https://doi.org/10.1007/978-1-4842-4950-5_2

The fact is that with intelligence activities there is no delimiting line that separates those which may be done under Title 50 or Title 10. The exact same information gathering activity could be performed under either title and still be completely above board and legal. The Secretary of Defense, for instance, has roles and authority to collect intelligence both under Title 50 and Title 10 legalities. In fact, Executive Order (EO) 12333 asserts this by directing that the Secretary of Defense be responsible for collecting intelligence for his Department of Defense as well as the Intelligence Community. Many members of the Intelligence Community are within the DoD such as the armed services (USA, USN, USAF, USMC), CIA, NSA, and NRO, while department members of the IC are not, such as Department of Energy (DoE), Department of Homeland Security (DHS), and Department of State (DoS).

The cyber domain may be equally leveraged by both titles and the DoD or IC. For example, the CIA or NSA as members of the IC may conduct computer exploitation to gain access to computer devices across the world in foreign intelligence efforts, and this activity would be considered to fall under Title 50 authority and its relating Intelligence Committee oversight. The exact same type of exploitation could occur against the same computer and for the same purpose of gathering intelligence but be performed by a uniformed member of the military under the direction of a military commander for the purpose of gaining situational awareness of a battlespace and be a Title 10 activity not needing Intelligence Committee oversight. The relationships between the Intelligence Community and Title 10 and Title 50 are depicted in Figure 2-1.

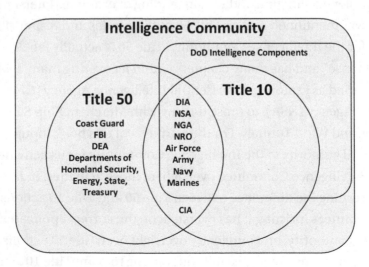

Figure 2-1. *Breakdown of Intelligence Community*

Title 10—Department of Defense

Among other things Title 10 actually outlines things like the uniformed code of military justice (UCMJ), as well as the establishment of the Departments of the Navy, Army, and Air Force. More relevantly to our discussions, it outlines roles and responsibilities of the Secretary of Defense (and the Commander in Chief through him) to conduct military activities. Therefore, the authority to conduct Title 10 activities is established as the Secretary of Defense and Commander in Chief, and the oversight for such activities is the responsibility of House and Senate Armed Services Committees. It is also important to understand that even though Title 10 activities are done with authority from the DoD, there is still a requirement for approval from Congress for the country to go to war. As such Title 10 activities of the DoD carried out against another state or otherwise declared enemy should require the same.

Interestingly, the Commander in Chief is allowed to deploy DoD assets on his or her own authority and discretion alone as long as Congress is notified within a 48-hour period. There is then a 60-day period where Congress must approve the action; otherwise, the activity must stop. These rules apply as much to cyber warfare under Title 10 as they do the deployment of troops. Something to consider here though is that at the end of 60 days, troops can be pulled back from a deployment or occupation. A missile battery can cease striking a target at the end of this same period even if the damage cannot be undone. The problem with certain aspects and tools within the cyber warfare realm is that at the end of 60 days there is in many cases no way to guarantee that a worm- or virus-type implement of war will stop performing its action. Such a tool may go on attacking systems of the target, or worse yet, bystanders and innocents, long after the 60-day period, and if Congress decides not to approve the action, then what?

Maintaining Military Operations

Congressional and House Intelligence Committees have in many cases asserted that it should have oversight of activities done under Title 10 via their intelligence oversight committees. This is especially true of cyber warfare given that it is conducted in secret and in places where public knowledge of such actions could raise both diplomatic and national security concerns. This contetion is understandable; however, the law outlines that as long as several requirements are maintained throughout the operation, it still falls within the boundaries of a Title 10 action. Cyber warfare activities are military actions by the DoD under Title 10 and not Title 50 actions of the IC so long as they remain under the control of a military commander and are performed before or during an actual or even anticipated military operation.

There are other restrictions as to what may be covered under Title 10 as a military activity; the following list attempts to capture them all at a high level:

- Must be conducted by US military personnel.

- Those personnel must be under command and control authority of a military commander.

- Activities must be either before or during ongoing or expected hostility where US military forces are involved.

- The role of the US military in that activity is obvious or will eventually be acknowledged publicly.

The first three were essentially already covered; however, the last one, that the role of the US military must eventually be admitted or obviously understood, is very interesting with regard to cyber warfare. Take the raid that killed Osama bin Laden, which was performed by military personnel in another sovereign country and without a declaration of war by Congress. This was done under Title 10 authority, and the reason it did not need approval from Congress is that the Commander in Chief at the time, Barack Obama, asserted his authority over the Department of Defense to order it and reported to Congress and in fact the world within 48 hours. The operation was already over so there was no need for Congress to even approve it within the 60-day window; also the raid was a Title 10 military operation and not a covert action, which we will cover later, due to the fact that the US military personnel role in it was acknowledged.

But hold on, the US DoD as well as IC devoted years of effort toward finding Osama bin Laden, how is it that the 60-day period was not long overdrawn? The answer is simply that many of the activities pre-dating the actual raid itself were carried out under Title 50 by the Intelligence Community. Where the waters get muddy for some with Title 10 and Title 50 here is the third item in the previous list which stated traditional military activities can be either before or during ongoing or expected operations involving military personnel. A type of activity that falls within the scope of this state is something called battlefield preparation, where under Title 10 authority, the DoD can do things like conduct reconnaissance, gather intelligence, and perform other actions of unconventional warfare which seemingly fall under Title 50 authorities as long as they are preparing the battlefield for conventional forces.

When we look at cyber activities that may relate to such a raid, we can clearly outline what falls under Title 50 and the oversight of Intelligence Committees and which does not. Most of the activity in the years, months, and even weeks prior to the raid in Pakistan are certainly within the realm of Title 50 authority and oversight. Intelligence was gathered, surveillance was conducted, and many other actions taken by the Intelligence Community. These activities can just as easily be performed within the domain of cyber, involving computer exploitation, as much as they can from space with satellites or in the air with drones and aircraft.

So, a computer that is attacked and taken over to perform surveillance of a target who may eventually be related to the raid is considered Title 50 and requires no special notification or approval from Congress. If cyber warfare is used to exploit computers that control communication systems or power systems with the intent of denying the enemy those resources once the operation began, it would fall under Title 10. These actions would be performed to prepare the battlefield for the Navy SEALs who performed the raid and would have to fall within that 48-hour notification and 60-day approval period as being traditional military activity.

Covert Action

So, what if the United States pursues actions and activity that isn't intelligence gathering, but that is never intended to be acknowledged and would be performed without military involvement? This type of activity as well as human intelligence efforts falls within the scope of US Code Title 50, Chapter 46, which covers the CIA specifically. As a note, there is also a slim potential that there could be times where the President may, though unlikely, direct elements of the DoD to conduct covert action. In such a case, the activity would be subject to the same oversight elements associated with normal Title 50 actions even though these could also be viewed as Title 10. Much like how military operations under Title 10 had specific requirements, so too does the non-intelligence-gathering activity of covert action under Title 50. Covert action must have all of the following attributes:

- An activity of the US government.

- Aimed at influencing political, economic, or military situations abroad.

- The role of the United States will not be obvious or ever acknowledged openly.

There are also several specific activities that do not fall within this purview of covert action. Covert action must not be any of the following:

- Activities with the primary goal of intelligence collection

- Activities with the primary goal of counterintelligence

- Traditional activities that are to better or maintain operational security of government programs or administrative activities

- Traditional diplomatic or military activities or their routine support

- Traditional law enforcement activities carried out by US law enforcement agencies or their routine support

- Activity that provides routine support to an overt activity

With all of the relevant activities discussed, Figure 2-2 represents how the different activities within Title 10 and Title 50 coexist.

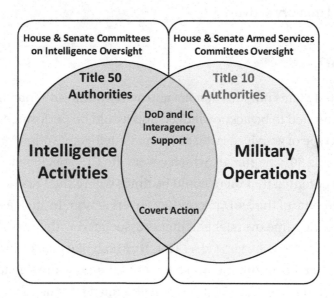

Figure 2-2. *Oversight and Activity Breakdown*

Bringing It Together

This has been a lot of policy and law that originally had nothing to do with cyber which is needed to understand the truly unique challenge it poses as a warfighting domain, a type of warfare, and a warfighting implement. Let's say another state discovers that their government and military computer systems have been infected by cyber tools such as virus or worm. Next, we will assume that by some extremely rare circumstance that state has reliably attributed that action to be done by the US military. In such a situation, that country would have no efficient way of knowing whether that computer was infected in an attempt to gather intelligence under Title 50 or to conduct military operations under Title 10. This creates an extremely precarious situation where a foreign government might choose to respond to an act of cyber-enabled intelligence gathering thinking that it was instead an act of cyber warfare because it could be nearly impossible to discern to which the activity was related.

Conversely, the United States itself would often be unable to determine whether or not the computer hacking attempts of other states were acts of war or intelligence gathering, assuming attribution somehow happened as well. As you can now see, it becomes extremely important where we draw the line between cyber-enabled intelligence gathering under Title 50 and cyber warfare under Title 10 as this will dictate how we respond as a nation to perceived cyber aggressions and how we avoid misrepresenting our intentions to foreign adversaries.

Known US Responses

We do not know the true extent of the US response to warfighting and other less belligerent but no less malicious activities within the cyber domain. It is likely facets of the response capabilities available to the National Security Agency (NSA) and US Cyber Command (CYBERCOM) will never see the light of day in an unclassified venue. This is obviously in the interest of national security and our ability to defend ourselves in the cyber domain. We do have several examples though of how the US federal government holistically responds to certain cyber threats, and it is at least worth noting how this is done and having a quick discussion on its ability to deter foreign actors.

Generally speaking, the only US responses to cyber activity we know about publicly are from various media, and government reporting on the indictment and may involve the charging of foreign actors involved in cyber domain activities. We will cover a multitude of different examples of what we would consider not Title 10 activities if the United States was conducting them. These activities were carried out against the United States in two rough categories of espionage and action that could be analogous to cyber warfighting activity. The participants in this activity are also far ranging in their implied relationship to state actions. It is also important to keep in mind while reading these examples that in none of these cases did a state government acknowledge the activity.

Example 1

The first example is an indictment of Chinese intelligence officers and their recruited hackers by US prosecutors in October of 2018. This is a very straightforward example of the type of activity that would be considered Title 50. There was a state-sponsored entity conducting intelligence gathering in efforts to steal sensitive but commercial aviation and technological data over the course of multiple years. The response by the United States upon attributing the activity to individuals was to charge both the members of the Chinese Ministry of Security as well as the apparent Chinese civilians they recruited to do the work.

Example 2

The second example is an indictment of two Chinese nationals by US prosecutors in December 2018. The attackers are attributed to hacking efforts against US government agencies and corporations which included the Navy and NASA. The attackers were said to be working for the Chinese spy agency, the Chinese Ministry of State Security. The activity is assumed to be something closely resembling what may be considered Title 50 actions as they were gathering information from agencies and corporations involved in aviation, space, and satellite technology. Since some of the targets involved were specific to the US Navy the cyber activity could potentially be perceived as battlefield preparation for a later kinetic or cyber attack against the US Navy by an aggressor state. If that was deemed the case, it could be then considered more like a Title 10 activity and a potential act of war in the cyber domain. Remember, there is essentially no way to differentiate between intelligence gathering for foreign intelligence efforts and cyber activity being conducted to prepare a battlespace.

Example 3

The third example is the only one we will discuss where the actual hackers themselves are attributed and identified as being uniformed members of a foreign state. The US prosecutors indicted five Chinese military hackers for cyber espionage against US corporations for commercial advantage. Here I think it is important to note that the charges filed were specific in the nature of the attack as being espionage and for commercial advantage and not related to anything that might be considered Title 10–type activity. Imagine a situation where it was military-uniformed hackers perpetrating activity like that in Example 2. There it might be a bit harder to argue against preparing the battlefield motive, and in that case, it could be even more easily considered a Title 10–type activity and therefore cyber warfare.

Example 4

The last example we will cover is one which has an end effect which could be most analogous to what a cyber war attack would look like but which has none of the other trappings required to be labeled or perceived as such. Iranian civilians without any connection to government or military assets of Iran were indicted by US prosecutors for deploying ransomware that affected many systems inside the United States by encrypting their files and not giving access back to the system owner unless a ransom is paid. Clearly this is not a warfighting activity as it was an orchestrated extortion scheme that lasted years and made hundreds of thousands of dollars. Where it does resemble cyber warfare is in the end effect. An activity in the cyber domain had effects which stretched into other warfighting domains. Targets of these attacks were government agencies, random companies, and also networks such as those belonging to hospitals. In fact, several hospitals were forced to close and turn away patients. Imagine if such an attack was in fact perpetrated by a uniformed member of a foreign government. It would almost certainly constitute a cyber warfare attack, and if it was heinous enough in its end effect, resulting in purposeful widespread loss of life, there is a chance such an attack could result in a declaration of war. If not that it is likely to invoke similar Title 10–like activity by the United States if the perpetrating state could be satisfactorily attributed and named.

Other types of activity in this category may have already occurred and either not been disclosed (or perhaps DoJ response is not what is used) or we have not noticed.

How does this impact our own actions? Imagine a foreign nation calling out the specific name of a uniformed military member who is operating within legal and operational authority and just war philosophy and international laws of warfare. What are the implications here, how do they factor in? Is this type of activity only okay when we are not in open declared war such as the simmering activities between the United States and Iran or China for instance?

We know two facts regarding the US response to cyber activity potentially related to other nation states. First, the US response to activity that does not resemble Title 10 activity, and thus is not considered cyber warfighting activity in the cyber domain, is addressed through indictment by the US Department of Justice. This is a response similar to what happens when foreign spies are identified within our borders, where they are indicted and arrested if found. The second fact of this response method is that it does little to deter foreign actors. In-person Title 50–like behavior within US borders means perpetrators risk capture. Cyber Title 50–like behavior by our enemies has little to no result on the perpetrator even when attributed by name.

As for the activity not represented in these examples, actual cyber warfighting activities perceived by the United States to be Title 10 type, we have no known responses by the US government. This either means that such actions are responded to in a way outside of DoJ indictment or that we have yet to undergo such attacks. Given the brazen activity such as that perpetrated by the Chinese, Russian, and Iranian state-sponsored actors, it seems that more likely than not these actions have been conducted against US targets, potentially attributed and responded to outside of the public eye.

The concerning point in all of this to me is that if other states react the same way the United States does upon attributing Title 50–like activity, we have risks to those serving our country in the uniformed services and greater Intelligence Community. Imagine being a member in the intelligence gathering apparatus of the United States as a young enlisted person and being asked as part of your legally ordered duties to collect intelligence on foreign nations. Then imagine that nation somehow attributed that activity to you and put your face and name on international news outlets indicting you for the crimes. You are now unable to travel internationally for fear of being arrested by countries or agents aligned to the charging state.

Often the perception on this indictment response is that it is essentially meaningless as a deterrent and often more symbolic than effective. However, when we turn the table and look at it as the United States is a perpetrator, we suddenly feel a sensitivity to the indictment of uniformed members following orders. There is a distinct difference between agents recruited and compensated by a state intelligence apparatus that willingly conduct Title 50–related cyber actions and those who are doing so as part of their obligated military duty. This is not necessarily directly tied to cyber warfare actions which this book addresses in whole, but I feel it is something worth pondering as we walk through the different implications in state-sponsored activity in the cyber domain, warfighting and otherwise.

Espionage

Because some of the examples covered previously mention espionage questions about where it fits in with Title 10 and Title 50, cyber warfare and intelligence gathering are certain to come up. I will do my best to cover this topic although it exists in an extremely undefined space with regard to legality and authority, especially in how the United States authorizes its agents to conduct espionage.

Defining Espionage

Merriam-Webster defines espionage as "the practice of spying or using spies to obtain information about the plans and activities especially of a foreign government or a competing company." To try and set apart this spying from what we have already established as information gathering we need to hone in on the mention of using spies. In my mind the difference between intelligence gathering under the authority that comes from Title 10 and Title 50 is that the perpetrator of that intelligence gathering is not a member of the state entity who wants the information.

This is not always the case, even just based on known espionage cases the United States has convened in court, but for the sake of differentiating espionage from intelligence gathering it is where I will draw the line. When the agent collecting information is a member of a state government or military and acting on that state's behalf, it should be considered as intelligence gathering for either Title 10– or Title 50– like efforts. When the agent collecting information is not a member of the collecting state but is recruited by members of the collecting state, they are considered to be performing espionage. Again, this is not a formal legal definition, but it is where I think a logical separation between the two and between the authorities lies.

Title 18

As the United States entered World War I, it established US Code Title 18, Chapter 37, to define espionage, likely in an attempt to prevent US citizens from breaking the henceforth established law to help enemies against the US government. The main focus of the articles under Title 18, Chapter 37, are in regard to activity where the individual is purposefully obtaining information about US national defense knowing that the information collected will be likely used to injure the United States in some way. Some articles cover protecting people perpetrating such acts and call out more specifics, but that is the overall gist of it.

So here we have a US law focusing on persons in the United States clearly outlining what we consider espionage. I believe it lends itself to the definition we covered previously. Transposing the two we essentially arrive at espionage is gathering defense information with the intent to injure the security apparatus of a state where the person collecting the information is within the state to be injured and the interested party in the conduct of the espionage an external state. One other interesting thing about espionage is that it is not always sponsored or recruited by the enemy state. In fact, in many cases of espionage in the United States, the person collecting information and passing it along to foreign powers did so of their own volition, sometimes out of spite and sometimes out of assumed financial reparation and for other philosophical and ethical motivations.

Cyber and Espionage

Where the activities covered by Title 10 and Title 50 have their own special applications in regard to the cyber realm and where authorities lie, in espionage this is not the case. Since the person perpetrating espionage is typically not a member of the state which will use that information to injure the target it is gathered against, trying to apply authority to it is not really useful. It would actually put the perpetrator in an awkward spot if it had defined legal authority for members of foreign states to act as agents on its behalf by conducting espionage. Further, espionage applies, as we said to the persons doing the spying. That spying may be conducted with a camera, notes, USB drive, computer hacking, or any number of tools. The tools and methods and domains used to conduct espionage do not affect the authority it is done through because it is ultimately considered to be not specifically authorized by law.

Summary

In this chapter we covered the legal authorities established by US Code that define the lines of conduct and who is responsible for the carrying out of given activities and who is responsible for their oversight. We have framed cyber warfighting and activity in the cyber domain under these laws so that we understand how they dictate the way in which cyber warfare may be carried out. This information also brought us to the powerful conclusion that apart from other methods of warfighting, the cyber domain makes it inherently difficult to distinguish whether an activity's motivation is related to warfighting or intelligence gathering. Lastly, we covered how the United States has officially responded to various activities by foreign agents in the cyber domain, noted the lack of any warfighting examples and discussed how espionage differs from authorized activity under US Code.

CHAPTER 3

Cyber Exploitation

When people generally speak of cyber-attacks or cyber warfighting, the onus typically seems to be on the end effect of the attack. This is understandable as the attack portion of cyber-attacks is usually a cyber-physical effect that even non-technical people can understand the impact of. When a cyber-attack can take control of a vehicle's braking and steering, for instance, the cyber-physical effect of the attack is what makes the news. To the non-technical, losing control of their vehicle is highly relatable. Whereas the hackers among us are more interested in how the vehicle controlling code was delivered to the vehicle and how it was able to take over those computing functions. The term cyber-attack is commonly conveyed and interpreted as the entire process of bringing the attack end effect to bear on a system. In actuality the process involves cyber intelligence gathering or reconnaissance, cyber exploitation, and then ultimately a cyber-attack effect.

In this same vein of common interpretation, the access needed to deploy the attack effect is almost entirely glossed over. This leads to wider spread interpretation issues primarily in military and policy circles. The focus in a military discussion tends to be exclusive to what end effect can be delivered to the enemy, and there is not enough respect for the sheer effort and technical capabilities needed to get that end effect delivered, if it is even possible to do so. Cyber-attack effects are a dime a dozen, but the ability to accurately find a target and then hopefully gain access to it can be tantamount to impossible. Imagine there was a mission to find some individuals home and then cause a bunch of damage to it to intimidate that person for beating up a friend of yours. Now, consider that the only information you have about the person was their nickname and that they would frequent a restaurant you know about while they were in town on work trips. Also, they beat up your friend yesterday, and if you can't damage their home in the next week, it is unlikely they will know that their house was trashed for beating up your friend. This doesn't seem like a mission that is very likely to succeed, does it?

If you can even determine where the person is travelling from on their work trips and who they were and then somehow find their address and get to it in the next week, that alone seems far-fetched. Suppose you somehow did though, you find their house

25

J. G. Oakley, *Waging Cyber War*, https://doi.org/10.1007/978-1-4842-4950-5_3

and you see they have camera systems and a dog and a sporadic work schedule. You want to trash the person's house for beating up your friend, but you also don't want to get caught, arrested, or bit, so now you need to figure out a way in; doing this as well in whatever time you have remaining in the week-long period is almost ridiculously unlikely. After all this effort to identify, locate, and sneak inside the person's home, it becomes rather trivial to find a way to cause destruction to intimidate the person. You could do any number of things, light a fire, smash Windows, dump garbage, and so on. The cyber warfighting activity process is just like this, appropriate reconnaissance can take time, and accessing the target can be nearly impossible and is constrained by a multitude of factors, time being only one of them. Once you have access to the target, much like access the home in our analogy, it is comparatively trivial to enact a noticeable cyber-attack effect.

A big reason for this is that, once access is gained, the attacker often is within the same or even a more privileged context than the normal users of the target. Security software and policies still need to let a user perform their needed actions on a given system and such have to make some assumptions that those on the device with appropriate context are supposed to be there. If security was such that it questioned every move of every user on them, they wouldn't be functional. This concept is similar to that of the process of clearing individuals with security clearances for work for the government and national security apparatus. At some point, once you have questioned and investigated the people and they have accessed a building with their badges and correct authority, there is an inherent trust that they are going to act as expected. Pieces of code on a cyber system are treated the same way. If after every security constraint and permission policy and filtering capability the code is still able to get onto the system and execute in a typical way, the system has to trust that it was not done maliciously.

Refined Definition

We have covered a lot of laws, policies, international agreements, and philosophical topics centered around warfare. We have inserted and analyzed how these institutions and ideologies affect cyber activity and the cyber warfighting domain. With the first two chapters as a frame of reference, I will clearly state my refined and appropriate definition for what constitutes cyber warfare before we delve into its technical specifics. This is necessary as we move forward through the technical chapters of this book and discuss how different aspects of technical cyber operations affect our ability to perform warfighting via the cyber domain. For an activity to meet my interpreted definition of being a cyber warfare action based on the previously discussed information, it must meet the following statements:

- The activity must originate in the cyber domain of warfighting.

- The activity must be covered by US Code Title 10.

- The activity must be conducted under the direction of a US military commander and not be an intelligence-gathering activity and be wholly within the cyber domain in preparation of the battlefield for a planned military operation or as part of an ongoing military operation by leveraging activity originating from the cyber domain to cause a noticeable effect in another warfighting domain (air, land, sea, space).

I will also take this opportunity to make a statement about how the United States could improve perception of its power in the cyber domain of warfare. We need our enemies to know, at least in part, what we are capable of. The United States is a feared power in the other warfighting domains because people can cite examples of that power. A nuclear attack submarine or destroyer, Tomahawk missiles, stealth bombers, and extremely talented special forces operators all convey US military power and themselves act as a deterrence, thus furthering the expectation of protection. Enemies of the United States know what it means if STRATCOM (Nukes) and SOCOM (Special Forces Operators) are brought against them, as well as the likely end effect. The role CYBERCOM plays in warfare is not known or established, so how can it help act as a deterrence?

Perhaps a small part of the reason foreign states are not deterred in conducting cyber acts against the United States is they do not know our ability to respond in the cyber warfighting domain. Maybe, if after a military operation, the role cyber activities played in it was acknowledged, it would help others perceive us as a leading player in cyber warfare. The United States readily admits when it launches Tomahawk missiles at targets in another country, why not start admitting when cyber is involved in Title 10 activity? After all, legally the United States acknowledges its role in Title 10 activity, and cyber warfare must fall within that legal authority.

I make no suggestion that this is easily done. I also must make clear that there are trade-offs in declaring that cyber warfare was involved in a wider military operation. The technical extant of this trade-off will be covered in the next chapter. I do believe though that to deter cyber warfighting against us, we in part must demonstrate our ability to wage war in the cyber domain. However, this must be done in a way that does not hamper or hinder our ability to continue to conduct warfighting or intelligence gathering activity in the cyber domain. Doing both may prove impossible, but it is certainly an interesting discussion to have.

Exploitation

We will first cover the activity of cyber exploitation as it is often required to perform both intelligence gathering and attack effect activity. Exploitation is also often referred to as remote code execution which is simply a technical way of saying the attacker is influencing the way a remote system behaves. I will caveat this by saying that there is also local exploitation to systems where access is already attained but that the context of that access does not have the privilege needed to execute the desired end effect of reconnaissance or attack. In either case, this is accomplished through leveraging a vulnerability. Just because a system has a vulnerability does not mean the attacker will be able to use that vulnerability to influence the way the remote system behaves. Exploitation or an exploit is the weaponization of a given vulnerability to gain that remote access necessary to alter the behavior of the remote system. Exploits are needed to deliver any cyber-attack effect, and when uniquely weaponized, they can take years and millions of dollars and scores of people to create, and when used even once, they are potentially identified by the rest of the world and then will be fixed and no longer usable, a fact which must be heavily weighed when deciding to utilize them.

Types of Exploitation

There are many different ways of exploiting systems in the cyber domain, and to understand the various challenges to exploitation in general, we will break them down categorically and cover examples of each type of exploit. Exploitation types are perhaps more accurately vulnerability types as the different factors that present a vulnerability to a system dictate how that vulnerability can be leveraged and the system ultimately exploited and accessed for deployment of attack effects.

Code Vulnerability

A code vulnerability is exploited by taking advantage of a flaw in underlying instructions that allows for remote manipulation of the system in a way that was unintended by the designers of the code. Exploitation of a code vulnerability often takes lots of work even when the vulnerability has already been discovered. Weaponization of a vulnerability is taking that unintended flaw and leveraging it in a purposeful and controlled way. Utilizing code vulnerabilities can many times lead to unwanted results. Sometimes leveraging a vulnerability may lead to remote access to the system, and sometimes it may result in a crash and power off of the remote system. Such a vulnerability is considered weaponized when it has a reasonable chance of attaining the intended result for triggering the vulnerability and an acceptable chance of unintended consequences.

As an analogy to this type of vulnerability, consider the following. Suppose you found out that if you wrote a destination address on an envelope with a first line that was longer than 20 letters and numbers, the mailman would assume it was incorrect and return it to sender. You also found out that the mailman never checked the return address when picking up your mail. These are two examples of vulnerabilities in the mail system. Figure 3-1 shows an example of a letter that has an acceptable 20 characters in the first line of the address (including spaces). This letter will be processed normally and sent to the correct destination address (1232 A. GOOD ADDRESS).

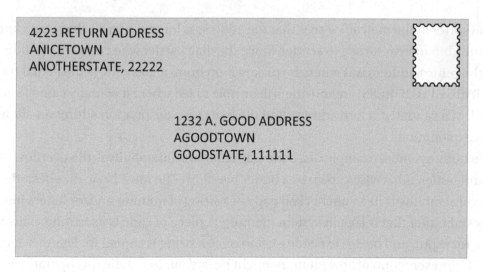

Figure 3-1. *Acceptable Letter*

Weaponizing the vulnerabilities involves combining them reliably for ulterior motives. For malicious reasons a terrorist wants to exploit these vulnerabilities and send someone anthrax through the mail and needs to make sure they don't get caught. The terrorist puts anthrax in the envelope with a 21 character destination (1232 A. FALSE ADDRESS) and a return address of the target of the anthrax (1337 TARGET ADDRESS) as shown in Figure 3-2.

Figure 3-2. *Rejected Letter*

The sorter at the mail office sees that the address is longer than 20 characters and puts it in a bin to be returned to sender. Since the mail carrier who picked it up didn't verify the return address was where he picked it up from, it gets sent to the actual target (1337 TARGET ADDRESS) and no one will be able to tell where it actually came from. The lack of a validated return address and the issue with destination addresses allowed for this exploitation.

The quintessential example of a code exploitation vulnerability is the overflow of an unbound buffer, otherwise known as a buffer overflow. The most basic manifestation of this vulnerability is in an unchecked copy of a string of number and/or letters into an unchecked buffer that is kept in system memory. A piece of code is executing, pauses waiting for input, and begins executing again once a string is copied in. Figure 3-3 shows a logical representation of how memory might be laid out to handle this operation.

Previous Code	Buffer	Address of Next Execution

Figure 3-3. *Logical Memory Layout*

Let's say the buffer waiting for the copied text can only hold four characters (ABCD) and that after that buffer is the eight characters that tell the computer the address in memory of what to execute next (54522345). Figure 3-4 shows an example of how this might look in our logical representation of memory for this simply function.

Previous Code	ABCD	54522345

Figure 3-4. *Example Memory*

If you copied 8 characters into the buffer during the string copy action, you would blow past the bounds of the buffer and overwrite the part that tells the computer what to do next as shown in Figure 3-5, where instead of copying the 4 characters ABCD, we copied the 12 characters ABCD12313371.

Previous Code	ABCD	12313371

Figure 3-5. *Overflown Buffer*

In this example the fact that there is no check to make sure the text entering the buffer is four or less characters is the vulnerability, allowing us to dictate what will execute next by overwriting the existing memory address (54522345) for the next thing the computer will process with our own specific location instead (12313371). If the 5th through 12th characters we copied in were the location of say something malicious we wanted to execute, then we have exploited that vulnerability to get the computer to execute code on our behalf.

Misconfiguration

Exploitation of a misconfigured system is pretty straightforward. The system has a setting or otherwise configurable option which has left it vulnerable. Weaponization of this type of vulnerability involves turning the misconfiguration into an ability to manipulate the target. Unlike code vulnerabilities, misconfigurations sometimes stand by themselves as an essentially weaponizable capability. Imagine a misconfiguration that allowed a remote entity to power off a system that controlled security cameras. In this case there is no further development to turn the misconfiguration into an attack effect like there likely would be if there was a code vulnerability in the same camera controlling system.

As an example of misconfiguration vulnerability exploitation, I'll use a facial recognition secured gate. After experiencing tons of false negatives where legitimate users were not being let through the gate, the security staff tuned down the sensitivity of the image detection that allowed individuals through after checking their face. This led to no more legitimate users being stopped at the gate, but it also meant that even those not in the facial recognition database were getting let through because the gate was no longer sensitive enough to tell the difference between most people. This is a misconfiguration that is allowing for a lot of false positives which is a dangerous result. A malicious individual could leverage this vulnerability to gain access to a building and sabotage something and the vulnerability itself required no weaponization for reliable exploitation, the individual simply walks up to the gate and is let through due to a false positive.

A relatable cyber system configuration vulnerability exploitation can be seen using the example of a misconfigured firewall. Firewalls are systems which filter incoming network traffic by acting on that traffic as it matches configured rules. Typically, the rules are in list form, and incoming traffic is compared against those rules either starting at the top and going down the list or vice versa. The safest way to configure a firewall is with a "deny all" as the last rule for comparison. This way, if traffic doesn't match an explicit "allow" rule on the list, it will ultimately be denied. Firewall rules can be unsafely configured for the same reasons as in our facial recognition gate in the previous example. If traffic getting filtered by the firewall is having too many false negatives and the system is not able to function, there is a possibility that the administrators of that firewall will begin to make the rules less strict so that everyday operations in the system are allowed to happen as intended. This also opens up the firewall to more likely have false positives as well, and a malicious actor may communicate through the firewall due to this. In the same way that the misconfiguration of the facial recognition gate did not need weaponization neither would the vulnerability present in the misconfigured firewall. The malicious actor is simply able to pass by the security feature due to its vulnerable configuration.

Human Mistake

To err is human. Exploiting the vulnerability of human nature itself is a technique everyone is familiar with and which translates well into the cyber domain. Weaponizing this type of vulnerability can be unnecessary and impossible when the vulnerability of a human mistake presents itself as a target of opportunity. On the other hand, planned solicitation of human mistakes can be pre-weaponized to take advantage of likely courses of human actions.

An example of an opportunistic human mistake vulnerability is as simple as tailgating behind a person after they badge into a secure area. The vulnerability in this example is that the individual with legitimate access to the secure area didn't make sure that the person behind them either also badged in or had to open the door themselves. There is not much weaponization potential for these kinds of human mistakes as they enable the attacker by chance. On the other hand, calling the phone number for technical assistance at a company and tricking the person on the other end of the call into divulging sensitive information will require some weaponization. The vulnerability here is the overly trusting human on the other end mistakenly giving up sensitive data. The weaponization of that vulnerability is turning that data into access to the company in some way.

Most are familiar with email phishing even they are not familiar with the term itself. It is the act of sending out emails that somehow trick the recipient into doing something. This example of cyber exploitation using the vulnerability of human mistakes is pre-planned and weaponized by already having some intended action or information to illicit from the recipients of the email. The email may tell the user that their bank password has expired and to visit a web site to reset it. The web site the user is directed to is set up by the attacker to log their credentials. The vulnerability is the human mistakenly thinking they need to reset their password and visiting the site in the email. The weaponization is the pre-built web site which logs the username and password they use so the attack can then access their bank account. An example of a target of opportunity type human mistake vulnerability in the cyber realm would be something like pulling up someone's email after they leave an internet café and forget to turn off or lock the computer they were using.

Illegitimate Use of Legitimate Credentials

This is the easiest to understand and simplest to leverage of the vulnerability categories, and exploitation of the vulnerability is similarly straightforward. In a non-cyber instance using legitimate credentials illegitimately, think of a house key. You go to your hardware store and they copy your house key for you while you shop. While they make you a copy, they also make themselves on and get your billing address when you pay with your credit card. The pattern on the key is a legitimate credential that will let you open the lock of your home when you get home. It can also be used illegitimately by the hardware store worker the next day when you are away to break into your house and take your belongings. The cyber domain also has keys, and they also can be copied by malicious actors for illegitimate use. This is the same for PINs and passwords as well. In some cases, especially in the software used to run devices like smart devices such as Wi-Fi-capable coffee machines or workout equipment, the passwords for the software is configured at a factory and almost never changed. When these credentials become public, they can be used by malicious actors to gain access to a device and from there target other systems. In all these examples, the vulnerability is clearly that legitimate credentials were obtained somehow and then the exploitation is using those credentials illegitimately to manipulate the behavior of another system.

Valuing Vulnerability Categories

To one degree or another, each of the vulnerability exploitation categories discussed in this chapter is caused by human error. Exploitation of human mistakes and utilizing valid credentials obtained through nefarious means require real-time errors by humans to facilitate remote manipulation of a system. Misconfigurations are human errors in the past which make a system more vulnerable than it could be if the system was correctly configured and code vulnerabilities are present due to a design-level error which becomes widespread through each instance of like systems.

Certainly, the value of a given vulnerability and its successful exploitation will vary from end effect to end effect especially to the warfighter more concerned with the attack portion of cyber activity. Exploitation-specific value however places the onus on a vulnerability's potential to allow for end effects whether those are Title 10 or Title 50 specific. In this sense human mistakes are the least valuable as the vulnerability presents itself often by chance and is typically no more immediately widespread than the individual who made the mistake. Slightly more exploitable than human mistakes are misconfigurations. This is because once discovered by an attacker, they can be repeatedly used.

Whereas a mistake like the one shown in Figure 3-6 might only lend itself to being leveraged the once, like our malicious email example, a facial recognition gate lets unintended people through can be used until the misconfiguration is identified. Misconfigurations are also likely to be shared among the same type of devices, especially in large networks where install or virtualization processes are likely repeated off a template, and if that template has a misconfiguration, it will be represented on all of the machines that use it.

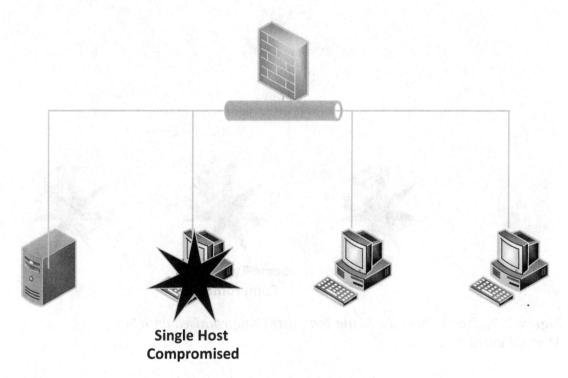

**Single Host
Compromised**

Figure 3-6. *A Single Host Compromised by Mistake*

Valid credentials would be more valuable for exploitation than either human mistakes or misconfigurations as once they were obtained it is likely they can continue to be used and also that they are potentially re-used on other systems from the same target set as shown in Figure 3-7. As an example, consider administrator credentials which are often re-used between systems at the same organization. Specifically, domain administrator credentials, for instance, can be re-used across any device in that domain, allowing one vulnerability to facilitate exploitation across a larger target set.

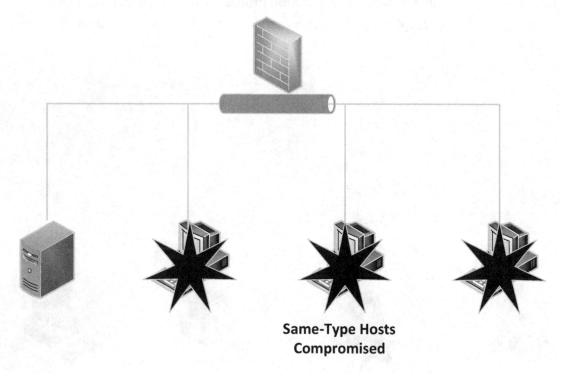

**Same-Type Hosts
Compromised**

Figure 3-7. *Hosts Using the Same Template Compromised with Same Misconfiguration*

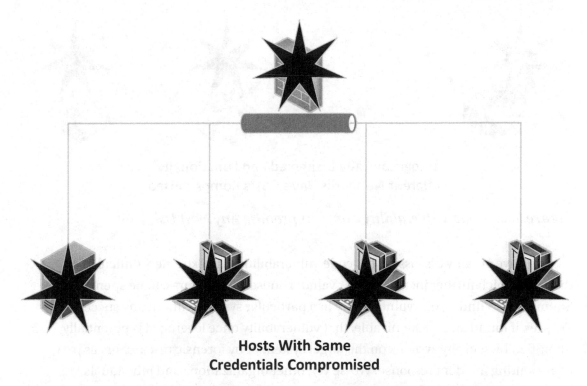

**Hosts With Same
Credentials Compromised**

Figure 3-8. *Credential Re-use Compromises Whole Network*

Most valuable of all are code vulnerabilities. They can be used more than once like valid credentials and misconfigurations until that use is discovered. Where misconfiguration vulnerabilities might be system specific and credentials potentially target set specific, code vulnerabilities apply to any organization using the software or system using that code. This means that once discovered a code vulnerability might allow remote manipulation of systems across the internet and not limited to a particular target set.

**Geographically Dispersed and Functionally
Different Networks Have Hosts Compromised**

Figure 3-9. *Code Vulnerability Can Compromise Any Host Using It*

We have already discussed that code vulnerabilities are extremely difficult to discover which further increases their value. Thousands of hours can be spent attempting to find a code vulnerability in a particular system without any success. Further, if found and weaponizable, that vulnerability once leveraged is potentially identified by security systems on the target system or by forensic researchers as part of a resulting incident response. Worse yet, other organizations and individuals are also constantly looking for unknown vulnerabilities in code across the spectrum of applications and software. Therefore, even if you found a code exploit that worked against systems you needed to target but you were holding off for an important enough end effect, someone else may have discovered it and leveraged it in some other effort. If someone else using the same or even a related exploit of a vulnerability similar to the one you have been holding on to, the response by the security industry may mean your exploit no longer works or is detected. The same is true for security researchers who are also looking for code vulnerabilities for bounty programs and even just as employment. All this means that good, weaponized code vulnerabilities should be used only after weighing the cost-benefit and careful tradecraft consideration to avoid being caught and the vulnerability discovered when able. It also means that part of this decision should be that there is always the potential that the exploit and vulnerability that has been created for military use could become known to the public and then potentially useless at any time as well. I will also cede the point that exploiting human mistakes or misconfigurations, though potentially limited to a specific system, may lead to the compromise of entire organizations. This focuses on the potential vulnerability those devices themselves pose to the organization if compromised and not the categorical cyber vulnerability that was exploited to gain access to them.

Title Implications

So, we must now ask ourselves which authority exploitation within the cyber domain happens under so that we know how it is affected by the non-technical constraints. As it turns out, the activity of cyber exploitation is used to enable both Title 10– and Title 50–type actions. It is fairly obvious that the end effect of cyber reconnaissance to gather intelligence falls within Title 50 authorities and that cyber end effect of attack activities falls within Title 10. Exploitation is often needed in either case, whether to gain access to the targets of intelligence gathering activity or to pre-position cyber-attack effects. The litmus for which authority cyber exploitation activities fall within is dictate by the intent for the follow-on cyber end effect. If cyber exploitation is performed to gain access to a device to garner intelligence, then that exploitation was done under Title 50 authority's subsequent oversight. Similarly if cyber exploitation allowed for an attack end effect tool to be installed on a system that was intended as a target of a military operation, it would fall under Title 10 as that exploitation would be considered battlefield preparation.

Summary

In this chapter we discussed the activity of exploitation within the cyber domain of warfighting. This activity leverages multiple different categorical vulnerability types and enables both the Title 50 end effect of intelligence gathering and the Title 10 effect of cyber-attack via battlefield preparation.

CHAPTER 4

Cyber-Attack

Cyber end effect activities fall into the two categories of cyber reconnaissance for intelligence gathering and cyber-attacks. The previously discussed activity of cyber exploitation is necessary in many cases to enable intelligence gathering and is always necessary for cyber-attacks. Some might argue that exploitation is not always needed to attack another system and that they could do things like denial-of-service attacks. An example of such an attack might be sending so much traffic to the target system that it cannot process it correctly and fails in some way. If we revisit our definition of exploitation though, and its purpose of manipulating the target system to cause behavior that benefits the attacker, we can see how attacks are in fact exploitation. If I am sending too much traffic for a routing system to handle and it fails over into an open state, allowing all traffic, or even if it just shuts down or stops processing traffic from other senders as well, then I have manipulated that system to behave in a way I wanted which means I exploited it.

As we discuss cyber-attacks, it is important to remember that they are always within Title 10 authority and oversight and they are also always intended to be noticed. The previous discussed cyber exploitation activity on the other hand is always intended to go unnoticed. The entity that is intended to notice the cyber-attack effect will differ, sometimes be the target and it will sometimes be the sender. Think about a cyber-attack that corrupts the hard drives where surveillance cameras are storing their recordings. This is an end effect that the aggressor probably does not intend, perhaps even hopes, is not noticed by the target. On the other hand, deploying malware that turns off power at enemy anti-aircraft missile battery locations is something that can't help but be noticed, though it if the target did not notice the sender is probably even happier. Lastly, there are cyber-attacks that are intended to be noticed by the target as a form of intimidation or other influencing action. This last type of cyber-attack, where the intent is for the target to notice, can be as far ranging as deploying malware that causes oil refineries to explode to malware that changes some form of state media to influence the populace of the target state. Though cyber-attacks are done as part of war and are acts of aggression, they can range considerably in their intended noise level as is illustrated by Figure 4-1.

© Jacob G. Oakley 2019
J. G. Oakley, *Waging Cyber War*, https://doi.org/10.1007/978-1-4842-4950-5_4

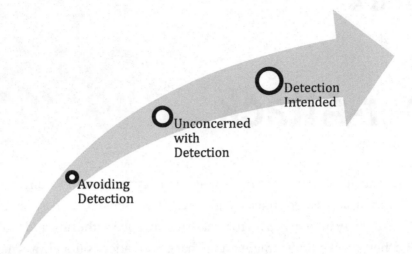

Figure 4-1. *Increasing Noise Level of Cyber-Attacks*

One final point to hammer home the difference between in exploitation and their related intent is that exploitation to prepare the battlefield by simply gaining access to a machine in preparation to launch an attack against it or other targets is done under Title 10 but not a cyber-attack. A cyber-attack is always done under Title 10 (just like launching a Tomahawk missile from a naval vessel is) and is always some form of cyber exploitation. It is also important to consider and acknowledge that there is no reason why a machine cannot be exploited under a Title 50 authority for the collection of intelligence and then at some later time that access can be used to deliver a cyber-attack effect to the target, attacking it or other hosts. Figure 4-2 shows a Title 10 cyber-attack from a host exploited under Title 10 to prepare the battlefield for launching that attack effect.

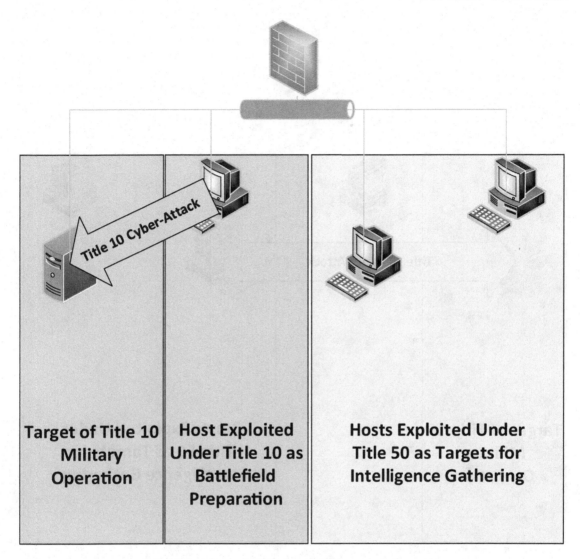

Figure 4-2. *Title 10 Attack Launched from a Title 10 Exploited Host*

In some cases, an outside organization from the military command wanting to target the system may already have internal access to the enemy state network being used for intelligence gathering purposes under Title 50. If the access is used to launch a Title 10 cyber-attack under the command of a military entity and is done in keeping with the other defining attributes of cyber warfare, it has been done legally and appropriately according to US Code dictating such behavior. This scenario is shown in Figure 4-3.

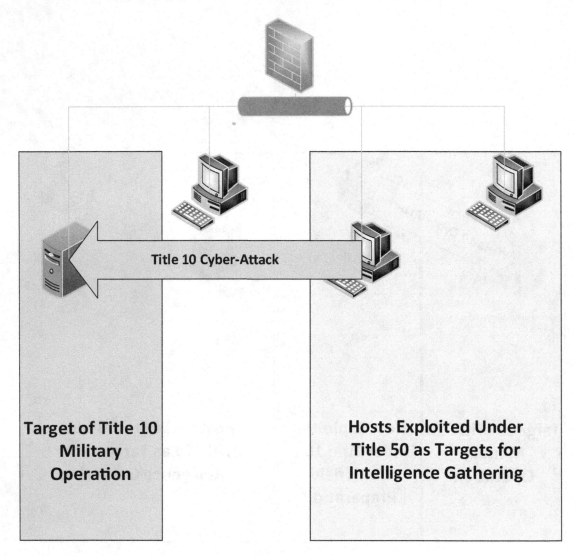

Figure 4-3. *Title 10 Attack Launched from a Title 50 Exploited Host*

Access to a target system can be legally obtained under the auspices of Title 10 or Title 50 behavior, it is only the operation that delivers and executes a cyber-attack effect that must be a Title 10 activity with meeting the full definition of cyber warfare. The relationship between access to exploited systems and the activity performed using that access is shown in Figure 4-4. It is worth noting that Title 10 exploited hosts for battlefield preparation should not be used for intelligence gathering as the authority for that exploitation activity was under the auspice that it was related to prepare for an imminent or ongoing military operation. Similarly, once access is turned over from Title

50 to Title 10 in preparation of a military operation and cyber-attack, it should not return to a Title 50 status for intelligence gathering. This is just my opinion, but if we look back at the dangers in confusing intelligence gathering activity with acts of war discussed earlier, we can see it might be a reckless activity with regard to risk of mis-attribution as further warfighting activity by the enemy state.

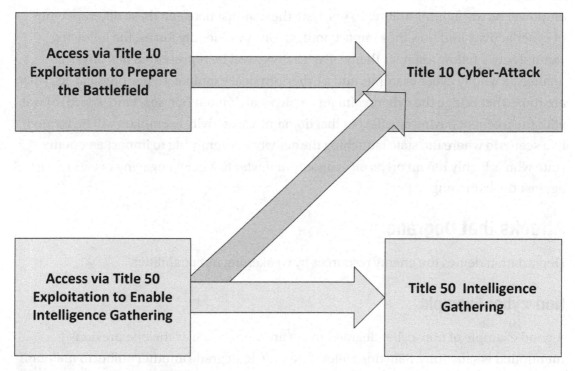

Figure 4-4. *Logical Relationships*

Attack Types

There are two types of cyber-attacks, those meant to deny something from the enemy and those meant to manipulate the enemy. Manipulation may not seem like an attack activity, yet if we consider the idea of an action being noticed by one entity or another and that that activity is not intelligence collection or battlefield preparation, it should be considered a Title 10 cyber-attack action, no matter how benign or impactful that noticeable end effect may be.

Denying the Enemy

Denying the enemy using attacks in the cyber domain falls within one of three categories of degradation, destruction, and disruption. The goal of these activities is to deny resources to the enemy which can be anything from terrain, troops, supplies, situational awareness, and essentially anything utilized by the enemy that could improve or empower its warfighting ability. To illustrate the contrast between these different types of cyber activity and how they impact both enemy and friendly forces, the following examples will follow a similar theme. Each activity will be represented in a physical analogy, a wholly cyber example, and a cyber-physical example. Cyber-physical activities are those that bridge the cyber realm into a physical domain (air, sea, land, space) of war with the intent of having an effect in that domain. The activity exemplars will be framed in a scenario where the state launching the activity is attempting to impact an enemy state who is highly reliant on its oil economy and who has been engaging in acts of war against the launching nation.

Attacks that Degrade

Degradation denies the enemy resources by weakening its capabilities.

Non-cyber Example

A good example of non-cyber degradation of an enemy such as the one previously mentioned is sanctions. Sanctions allow one state to degrade another ability to maintain economical might and governing stability. Against an enemy highly reliant one type of good to maintain both its economy and government, restricting the ability for that nation to market, sell, and profit from its resource can be highly impactful and is often a priority tactic compared to other more violent physical degradation options.

Cyber Example

The headquarters of the state-owned oil company has a large firewall that manages connections to all external assets such as refineries and drilling rigs. The aggressor state sends heavy amounts of network traffic at the external points of presence reachable from the internet. The traffic is so much that it makes the firewall drop communications. The ability to communicate over the network becomes so bad for the state-owned oil company that it has to resort to telephone calls, in-person hand-offs of information, and transmission of orders to external assets by mail and messenger. This severely degrade the ability for the state to operate is most important resource.

Cyber-Physical Example

The aggressor state might target the drilling rigs that the enemy state uses to produce its oil and fund the rest of its efforts as a nation. To do this and cause degradation, the attacker might be utilizing a cyber weapon that uses the cyber domain to affect the physical. If a virus could alter the speed control for the drills used to find and pump oil, it might make those drills less efficient and make it harder for the enemy to garner more resources. It also may make the drill heads more likely to break and need replacement which would further degrade the state's oil production.

Attacks that Disrupt

Disruption denies the enemy resources by interrupting or stopping enemy activities.

Non-cyber Example

In the scenario we are discussing a physical example of disrupting the enemy would be to blockade the port or ports from which the enemy transports its oil. Doing so doesn't destroy any of these assets, which can be valuable as they could be utilized later by the attacking state. This could be considered a more effective way of denying resources to the enemy state than a degradation effort, but it is also much more overt and likely to lead to outright armed conflict with kinetic weapons. This type of disruption also has the added bonus of potentially hemming up the enemy state naval forces as well as they would be prevented from leaving port where they are vulnerable or returning to port for supplies if they were out at sea.

Cyber Example

A cyber domain disruption of this enemy could be manifested by attacking the enemy state's ability to leverage global finances and move its valuable oil products to garner other resources. In this effort the attacker state launches a cyber-attack tool which was able to infect the state computers which access and participate in global stock exchanges. Once installed, the tool aims to ensure no stock purchase or sale requests made reach the exchanges. This disruption would severely hamper the ability of the enemy state to maintain economic stability, putting great pressure on the government.

Cyber-Physical Example

Instead of using naval vessels to blockade enemy ports, a cyber-physical disruption would consist of something with similar end effect but enabled through the cyber domain. Here, a cyber-attack tool could be delivered to the enemy oil tankers trying to leave the port loaded with oil. This cyber-attack tool takes control over engine or navigation controls and is used to either make the tankers dead in the water or cause them to steer in gentle circles. In this attack, the assets aren't destroyed and are available for the attacker to potentially use later, but the disruption of shipping oil from the port is also achieved.

Attacks that destroy

Destruction is relatively straightforward and easy to understand; this attack effect denies the enemy a resource by destroying it.

Non-cyber Example

There are any number of destructive capabilities in many state arsenals, but in keeping with the theme of these examples, the physical destructive example I would cite is the destruction of enemy oil refineries using sea to land based missiles. The destruction of oil refineries limits the potential for loss of innocent lives or widespread ecological disaster by striking targets already kept far from civilian areas due to its inherent dangers and whose oil lines can eventually be shut off. Conversely, striking something like an oil tanker is not only likely to cause loss of innocent lives but would also lead to huge ecological impacts.

Cyber Example

Keeping a destructive denial of resources entirely within the cyber domain while still being effective requires slightly more creativity than our other examples. If the attacker could identify and gain access to all locations where sales, shipping, and production logs were kept for the state-owned oil company and then summarily corrupt or encrypt all of those digital files, it could potentially lead to a significant denial to the enemy state as it is likely that most transactions are completely carried out and stored in the cyber domain. Even were this not the case, the attack would still be effective in compromising the state's ability to do business with its state-owned oil company.

Cyber-Physical Example

For a cyber-physical effect, let's consider an example that again results in a similar impact to the physical example but which is cyber enabled instead of due to the damage caused by a missile. The attacking state might try and deploy a virus that alters the way the oil refineries maintain gas and liquid pressures in the refinement systems with the goal of causing them to fail catastrophically. The end goal of destroying refineries is accomplished but with a less likely violent reaction by the enemy state.

Manipulating the Enemy

Though the previously discussed denial attacks seem to represent what might be called a classic example of cyber-attacks, manipulation of the enemy using attacks within the cyber domain can be just as useful in warfighting. I won't attempt to come up with my own definition for what this manipulation is defined as. Joint Publication 3-12: Cyberspace Operations put out by the military members of the Department of Defense, dated June 2018, states that manipulation attacks are defined as follows:

> *Manipulation, as a form of cyberspace attack, controls or changes information, information systems, and/or networks in gray or red cyberspace to create physical denial effects, using deception, decoying, conditioning, spoofing, falsification, and other similar techniques. It uses an adversary's information resources for friendly purposes, to create denial effects not immediately apparent in cyberspace. The targeted network may appear to operate normally until secondary or tertiary effects, including physical effects, reveal evidence of the logical first-order effect.*

I think this definition very refined and also, coming in the form of warfighting doctrine from a nation state's military, is topically representative of what we can expect from this type of cyber-attack. I find it useful to categorically break this type of attack into two different types, each having two varied intentions. There are manipulation attacks which alter the indicators a system is showing and thus the perception of a human interpreting the system wouldn't be based on reality. There are also those that manipulate a system's ability to perceive inputs as designed which also would ultimately misrepresent reality to the human interpreting it. This second type of manipulation is broadly termed as sensor perception compared to the human perception. In either case, manipulation attacks can be done for aggressive or protective reasons. Aggressive manipulation of human or sensor perception is done to enable attack effects against the enemy. Protective manipulation on the other hand is done to protect the warfighting resources of the attacker whether they be lives of troops or cyber tools.

Human Perception: Aggressive

The following are examples of manipulation of human perception for aggressive means.

Non-cyber Example

Some may argue that influence operations are outside the scope of military activity and fall more within the realm of espionage. I believe that as long as the goal of such influence is not to overthrow the local governing parties and is directed toward adding military operations, it does still fall within Title 10 activity, especially when we consider the battlefield preparation clause. As a physical example of this, imagine the attacking state dropped flyers from airplanes much like was done in World War II by both the allies and the axis forces. If these flyers said that oil refineries were going be struck by missiles in 2 days, it could be done with two potentially effective impacts on the enemy.

First, the enemy might lose resource production capabilities as people were afraid to work at the oil refineries even if no attack was launched, which has nearly the same outcome as if they were actually attacked. Second, this could be a distraction as the attacker actually planned to attack oil lines that transport the oil from the refineries to customers. This second benefit might be considered more protective than aggressive though as it distracts resources from defending the actual target of a strike.

Cyber Example

A completely cyber domain contained example of a manipulation attack might involve state social media accounts and other state dissemination capabilities. The attacker would want to gain access to these systems with the goal of changing the language of what is posted via these capabilities as an attack on the enemy state. This could be done by changing information put out by the state attempting to calm and ensure order to statements that are incendiary and instill insecurity in the populace. The enemy state may be saying everything is fine with the economy and there were no financial issues in an attempt to maintain economic and governing stability. If the attacker changed that to posts saying if issues with oil resources go on for even a few more days there might be economic collapse, it could certainly have an aggressive impact on the enemy state.

Cyber-Physical Example

A cyber-enabled effect for a manipulation of human perception might be something as simple as making all danger indicators for oil pipelines and refineries constantly stay green despite what sensors are reading. The underlying systems are still performing their job and identifying danger situations, but instead of conveying that accurately, the indicators perceived by the systems are constantly showing that there are no issues. This combined with other affects could lead to extremely effective attacks against such systems without humans realizing until failure was catastrophic. Even in the absence of other attacks against these systems, there remains the possibility that they fail on their own and that the humans who are supposed to monitor them would be unaware until something destructive occurred to indicate there was an issue.

Human Perception: Protective

The following are examples of altering human perceptions through attacks for protective reasons.

Non-cyber Example

Going back to World War II, we can find another classic example of manipulation of human perception, and this time to protect attacker resources. Using wood and other materials, troops constructed fake tanks so that observers from a distance or in the air would think that tank units were deployed in an area they were not. This means that the enemy is less likely to keep looking for other tank units and would likely waste their own resources engaging these fake tanks. This might allow the real tanks to gain better position or successfully engage enemy forces.

Cyber Example

Protecting the attacking state forces from the enemy is also well accomplished completely within the cyber domain. Imagine the attacking state had advanced forces in the country behind enemy lines, and those forces who are currently operating in a covert nature prior to the military operation think they were caught on security cameras. If the attacking state had access to the network those cameras were on and was able to replace the camera recordings that potentially captured the advanced forces with copies of ones where nothing was going would be an example of a cyber manipulation in the cyber realm to prevent the enemy's ability for human perception to identify the advanced forces.

51

Cyber-Physical Example

Let's say that the cyber example was not completely successful and one of the advanced operatives was captured by local law enforcement and needs immediate rescue before it is determined he was from the attacking nation and was placed at risk to grave harm to himself and potentially divulging damaging information about the attacking state's operations as well. A cyber-physical attack could be used to leverage cyber accesses in the police headquarters where the operative was being held as part of rescue efforts. For instance, if the attacking state was able to use access gained via cyber exploitation to execute a cyber-attack that set off all the fire alarms at all police stations in the city of the state police headquarters, it would cause enough commotion and confusion to make it safer and easier for special forces operators to infiltrate and rescue the captured operative. Here the human ability of the enemy state to perceive what was really going on and adequately respond to the rescue attempt of the attacker operative was successfully manipulated.

Sensor Perception: Aggressive

The following are examples of manipulation of sensor perception for aggressive means.

Non-cyber Example

A very literal and non-cyber way of interacting with enemy sensors in an aggressive activity could be using mobile lasers to remotely heat sections of oil pipeline in remote locations of the enemy state. This would cause sensors to incorrectly think there was a dangerous issue and either shut down parts of the oil distribution network or require response by human inspectors. Either way the operation is an attack on the oil distribution network by abusing the sensor's ability to detect heat as an indicator of danger.

Cyber Example

A cyber example of aggressively attacking a sensor's ability to perceive and thus relay correct information could be an attack against laboratory devices belonging to the enemy state-owned oil company. In this situation malicious code attacks and alters the controlling functions of different measurement and detection devices within the oil company laboratory in an effort to have them develop flawed formulas that they believe in the lab to be improvements which in fact make their important state reliant resource worse. This type of attack could also interfere with the sensor's ability to read quality measurements from different oil products and, by altering the sensor's ability to measure quality, impact the company from preventing poor product, making it to markets and impacting their reputation as a provider and exporter. This example is holey cyber since the attack on the sensors happens via the cyber domain, and the end effect is the laboratory producing data into the cyber domain that is inaccurate and potentially disastrous to the enemy state.

Cyber-Physical Example

There are many examples of how altering the ability of a sensor to correctly read its target metrics could lead to issues of a cyber-physical nature. One such might be infecting the ballast control software for the enemy state oil tankers with malware that makes the ballast and list sensors of the tankers report read inaccurately. This type of attack could lead to oil tankers rolling from side to side or sinking too deep in shallow waters and running aground. This attack could thus be a manipulation of sensors in an aggressive way that leads to either destruction, by leading the tankers to run aground, or a disruption in causing them to roll uncontrollably and prevent them from taking on their cargo or transporting it, out of the port. If done in a more controlled and less noticeable manner, this manipulation of sensors could also degrade by making the tankers much less efficient due to ballast instability in their travel to offload the enemy state's export of oil.

Sensor Perception: Protective

The following are examples of altering human perceptions through attacks for protective reasons.

Non-cyber Example

Suppose the attacking state needs to drop ordinance from jets to destroy assets of the enemy state either in preparation for or party to a military invasion. The enemy state likely has anti-aircraft capabilities such as surface to air missiles. In this scenario the jet may launch chaff or flak upon detection of a surface to air missile launch in hopes of distracting the missile and protecting the jet. This is a non-cyber example of protectively influencing sensor protection. The missile was homing in on the attacker jet before the anti-missile capabilities drew the missile away from the jet, saving the pilot and aircraft and allowing it to drop its ordinance on the target.

Cyber Example

Just as bomb dropping aircraft may need protection entering enemy airspace, cyber-attack activities may need assistance entering enemy cyberspace. There might be enemy firewalls sniffing and identifying traffic that would prevent both battlefield preparation and even more dire cyber-attack effects as a war with an enemy state continued. If an attack tool was uploaded to the firewall post-exploitation that could alter the ability of that firewall to pick up on just the attacker's traffic, it would be an example of a cyber effect on sensor perception to protect the ongoing and future operations. Instead of leveraging a misconfiguration or altering the enemy system to make it misconfigured, this type of attack might affect the enemy firewall device at a lower level such that its ability to see specifically the attacker traffic is nullified, but to the managers and administrators of that firewall, all rules and configurations would continue to look correctly in place because they had not been modified.

Cyber-Physical Example

Bridging the gap between these scenarios to a cyber-physical affect could be an effort to attack radar systems. These are complex systems and are reliant on extremely tailored sensors as well as computing systems. The attacker may want to mitigate detection by the enemy state radars by using a cyber-attack to manipulate the ability of the radar system to read radar signatures of larger objects, instead interpreting them incorrectly as bird-sized objects. In this case the radar system affected by a cyber-attack tool would be relaying what it perceived as accurate information to the human monitors that the incoming objects were birds and not attack helicopters.

Espionage

Some of the examples given, especially those falling categorically under the manipulation type of cyber-attack, certainly come close to the line between cyber-attack activities under Title 10 and what may be considered espionage. Firstly, the individual conducting the act has a large part to do with it. Uniformed members of the armed services, particularly in the United States, are typically not authorized to perform espionage activities. More certainly, if they did, even through cyber means, it would have to be under the command and direction of some other entity besides the Department of Defense.

Let's take the grayest example in a world that is not really black or white anyways. We discussed an example of cyber-attack activity where the attackers were manipulating message boards, social media, and other mediums. In a situation where this effort ties in some way to a military operation, be it short in duration or a long-standing invasion, it can be considered safely within the Title 10 authority of cyber-attack via manipulation against an enemy state. It becomes espionage when the efforts of that social media manipulation are aimed at sowing discord and upheaval in the enemy state's inhabitants in hopes of overthrowing or altering or weakening that state's government and/or national defense capabilities.

Summary

In this chapter we discussed in depth the cyber domain warfighting activity of cyber-attack and provided numerous analogies as teaching points for the categorical differences in types of cyber-attacks. The difference in both traditional warfighting and unconventional cyber warfighting was discussed in respect to both denial and manipulation categories of attack. Scenarios were used to show the differences between degradation, disruption, and destruction cyber-attack operations and similarly used to illustrate both aggressive and protective manipulation attacks against the perception of both human and sensors. Lastly, we discussed how espionage in the cyber domain can seem similar but is motivationally different than cyber manipulation activities.

CHAPTER 5

Cyber Collection

The last cyber activity involved in waging war within the cyber domain is intelligence gathering which is integral to the success of any military operation. Whether it is done to support a Title 10 military operation of general national defense purposes supporting situational awareness, intelligence gathering is strictly a Title 50 effort. Unlike cyber-attack activity, intelligence gathering does not always rely upon cyber exploitation as an enabler.

According to the US Department of National Intelligence (DNI) which oversees the Intelligence Community, there are six methods of intelligence gathering. Listed as follows are the definitions straight off the DNI official government web site[1]:

> *SIGINT—Signals intelligence is derived from signal intercepts comprising -- however transmitted -- either individually or in combination: all communications intelligence (COMINT), electronic intelligence (ELINT) and foreign instrumentation signals intelligence (FISINT). The National Security Agency is responsible for collecting, processing, and reporting SIGINT. The National SIGINT Committee within NSA advises the Director, NSA, and the DNI on SIGINT policy issues and manages the SIGINT requirements system.*

> *IMINT—Imagery Intelligence includes representations of objects reproduced electronically or by optical means on film, electronic display devices, or other media. Imagery can be derived from visual photography, radar sensors, and electro-optics. NGA is the manager for all imagery intelligence activities, both classified and unclassified, within the government, including requirements, collection, processing, exploitation, dissemination, archiving, and retrieval.*

---

[1]www.dni.gov/index.php/what-we-do/what-is-intelligence

© Jacob G. Oakley 2019
J. G. Oakley, *Waging Cyber War*, https://doi.org/10.1007/978-1-4842-4950-5_5

MASINT—Measurement and Signature Intelligence is technically derived intelligence data other than imagery and SIGINT. The data results in intelligence that locates, identifies, or describes distinctive characteristics of targets. It employs a broad group of disciplines including nuclear, optical, radio frequency, acoustics, seismic, and materials sciences. Examples of this might be the distinctive radar signatures of specific aircraft systems or the chemical composition of air and water samples. The Directorate for MASINT and Technical Collection (DT), a component of the Defense Intelligence Agency, is the focus for all national and Department of Defense MASINT matters.

HUMINT—Human intelligence is derived from human sources. To the public, HUMINT remains synonymous with espionage and clandestine activities; however, most of HUMINT collection is performed by overt collectors such as strategic debriefers and military attaches. It is the oldest method for collecting information, and until the technical revolution of the mid- to late 20th century, it was the primary source of intelligence.

OSINT—Open-Source Intelligence is publicly available information appearing in print or electronic form including radio, television, newspapers, journals, the Internet, commercial databases, and videos, graphics, and drawings. While open-source collection responsibilities are broadly distributed through the IC, the major collectors are the DNI's Open Source Center (OSC) and the National Air and Space Intelligence Center (NASIC).

GEOINT—Geospatial Intelligence is the analysis and visual representation of security related activities on the earth. It is produced through an integration of imagery, imagery intelligence, and geospatial information.

Cyber Intelligence Gathering

Though not called out specifically, intelligence gathering within the cyber domain logically falls under the SIGINT method of intelligence gathering. The interesting thing about cyber intelligence gathering under the SIGINT discipline is that it allows intelligence gatherers to potentially gather intelligence that correlates to each of the six disciplines. For instance, in accessing enemy computer systems and conducting cyber intelligence gathering, images might be found stored on the computer system, tying SIGINT and IMINT together. It is also possible that measurements and technology documentation about enemy systems could be found on computing systems of the enemy, tying SIGINT and MASINT together. If the cyber domain was used to solicit human sources via social media and other digital mediums, it would tie HUMINT to SIGINT. If the cyber domain was leveraged to gather information from foreign state news web sites, it would tie SIGINT to OSINT. If cyber activity was used to gather data from the foreign equivalent of Google Earth pictures, maps, and geolocation of a foreign adversary location over time to put together an understanding of that adversary, it would tie SIGINT and GEOINT together. This matrixing of intelligence mediums is unique to cyber intelligence gathering.

The Department of National Intelligence also outlines on their web site that there is a routinely updated National Intelligence Strategy (NIS) outlining a prioritization of intelligence gathering activities for the whole Intelligence Community. As part of this NIS is the listing of objectives for IC intelligence gathering. The first three of these objectives are foundational and unchanging in the charter of the DNI's NIS charter to the IC. These three objectives are as follows:

> **Strategic Intelligence**—*inform and enrich understanding of enduring national security issues;*

> **Anticipatory Intelligence**—*detect, identify, and warn of emerging issues and discontinuities;*

> **Current Operations**—*support ongoing actions and sensitive intelligence operations.*

Something that stands out regarding intelligence gathering in the cyber domain under the SIGINT discipline is that for any intelligence gathering that needs to be enabled by cyber exploitation, there is a need to have prior intelligence gathering to determine how to accomplish that exploitation against intended targets. I will refer to this activity specifically as cyber reconnaissance, which is meeting the third objective of supporting current or ongoing operations. Here, the intelligence doesn't necessarily serve a strategic need of the IC or even benefit anything outside of the current intelligence gathering operation as it is used to survey the attack surface of the target within the cyber domain to determine best paths of increase access and in furtherance of operational goals.

Cyber intelligence is therefore any intelligence gathered in the cyber domain that will help target additional assets or garners information for strategic or anticipatory objectives, and cyber reconnaissance is specifically intelligence gathered from a target that is used to exploit and access cyber systems. Cyber reconnaissance is also necessary in any exploitation utilized to prepare a battlefield for or simply execution of cyber-attack activities, as there is a need for information that will lead to targeting and successful attacking of enemy assets. There is no difference in authority as both the gathering of cyber intelligence and the performance of cyber reconnaissance are under Title 50, the difference is the customer of the data being gathered. Cyber reconnaissance data furthers a cyber domain operation and is likely consumed most importantly by the entity conducting that cyber domain operation. Cyber intelligence is gathered for the customers who are likely to perform intelligence analysis.

Figure 5-1 shows the logical representation between reconnaissance, exploitation, and intelligence gathering in the cyber domain. Once a target has been determined to likely contain intelligence, cyber reconnaissance is performed to determine how it might be exploited, exploitation gives access to the system using one of the identified vulnerabilities, and then intelligence gathering efforts commence on that target.

Figure 5-1. *Cyber Domain Intelligence Collection*

Figure 5-2 shows a logical representation of the relationship between cyber intelligence collection, cyber reconnaissance, and cyber-attack. Here, intelligence was gathered that identified the appropriate target for the attack, cyber reconnaissance was used to determine what vulnerability would enable the attack effect, and then the cyber-attack can be executed.

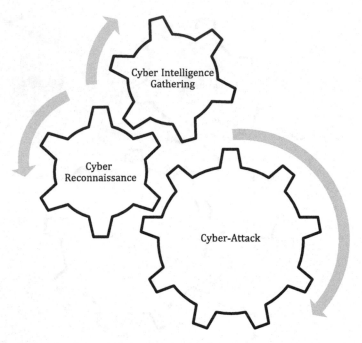

Figure 5-2. *Cyber Domain Cyber-Attack*

Cyber Domain Collection Examples

Just as we did with exploitation and attack activities, I will walk through some different examples of intelligence gathering to really drive home an understanding of what it looks like when performed in the cyber domain. I have split these examples into four operationally different efforts of cyber intelligence gathering.

First and foremost, cyber intelligence gathering can be done using the discipline of OSINT or open source intelligence, which is the obvious example for intelligence gathering that does not require exploitation as the sources of OSINT information are publicly available. Cyber intelligence gathering can also take on the methodology of HUMINT when the cyber domain is simply the conduit between the requester of the HUMINT and the source. Instead of meeting in a dark alley to exchange information or approach potential sources, it can be done more safely and anonymously through the cyber domain.

The last two types of cyber intelligence gathering operations are directed and indirect. Directed is the purposeful collection of specific information from any of the six disciplines off of a target cyber system. Indirect cyber intelligence collection is any effort aiming to collect data about cyber systems but not from them which is also known as metadata. Metadata is simply data that tells information about other data.

To understand this concept, think of a delivery truck. The data in question, or rather the intelligence needed, is what the delivery truck is carrying inside. Opening the backdoors to the truck would certainly let you know what the cargo was and that would be direct data gathering. Indirect data gathering would be looking at information about the truck such as its speed, direction of travel, how low it is riding on its suspension, what is written on the side, and other details that can be used to help determine what it might be carrying. These are examples of metadata collected indirectly.

The following collection examples will mostly maintain the theme of an enemy with extremely important oil interests.

Open Source Collection

Open source collection is that which requires no special access or authorization and can be collected from publicly available sources.

Non-cyber Example

Overt observation is the most straightforward example of OSINT. The target is in no way attempting to disguise or camouflage something, and the observer is in a location and context that required no extraordinary enabling efforts such as illegally entering a country or sneaking into a secure area. To accomplish OSINT collection against the oil-dependent enemy state, an agent takes an extended vacation to a country that shares a bay with the enemy. Weekend after weekend the agent charters fishing boats in the bay which is also home to the main oil port of the enemy state. The agent hasn't illegally entered the neighboring state and simply takes photos every weekend during fishing charters to build a pattern of life about the oil tankers coming and going from the enemy port to potentially aid in targeting them for escalated action.

Cyber Intelligence Example

Using OSINT in the cyber domain to gather intelligence about the enemy state is very similar. The agent uses publicly available data from stock market tracking web sites to monitor the activity of the stock listing for the enemy state-owned oil corporation. Over a long period of time and gathering many data points, this type of intelligence could lead analysts to determine that every February there is a huge surge in stock activity with the state-owned oil corporation holdings for one reason or another. This could be used to time a cyber-attack against the corporation when it seasonally has the highest amount of stock activity to cause the most financial and reputational damage.

Cyber Reconnaissance Example

OSINT can be very valuable for exploitation efforts aimed at gaining access to enemy systems within the cyber domain. Surprisingly organizations often publish on their web site or even in news media that they have just undergone a technology upgrade and sometimes more details than should be divulged. Imagine the enemy state announces they have upgraded their entire stock exchange systems to facilitate faster trading and that they are using the latest of a certain brand of server to process trades quicker. They also state when the install began and that it was just finished. An attacker may be able to determine that based on the model and when they were installed what the operating system version is and be able to research vulnerabilities to leverage against the system. Worse, an attacking nation state with the time and resources might just go buy the same hardware and install the same software likely to be on that hardware based on the dates in the article and do their own reverse engineering to find new vulnerabilities.

Human Source Collection

HUMINT using human assets to ascertain intelligence is very close to espionage just as manipulation attacks are also similar in conduct. The focus of distinction is again on the motive and goal. HUMINT can be very overt, when done under Title 10 in preparation of a battlefield. Here, a likely uniformed military member may ask a human source to come back in the morning with a count of how many enemy combatants were seen entering a complex during the night to better prepare to attack that facility.

Under Title 50, more covert agents or handlers are managing assets to gather intelligence inside and against the enemy state. In this situation the covert handler may ask the human asset who owns a food stand to return and give information such as car type, clothes worn, and so on when a certain person is seen in a market to help target that individual for further intelligence gathering or kinetic actions. Espionage would be having a covert agent or handler ask their human asset to start a rally in the enemy state capitol to try and get a violent response out of the government and increase sympathy in the enemy state for rebellion with the eventual goal of toppling that government.

Non-cyber Example

A non-cyber, traditional HUMINT example concerning our overall theme would be having local farmers with land along roads to main oil distribution centers keep track of how often, how many, and what direction oil shipments using truck are headed and reporting back with that information on some regular basis. This type of information can be used to learn more about potential production and sales levels as well as lead to better targeting of oil distribution centers for better effect than would be accomplished without such information.

Cyber Intelligence Example

To gather intelligence using human assets in the cyber domain, an often-frequented source of information is likely chat rooms and message boards. In this example the handling party would look for a source who was willing to participate in these forms of communication with actors from the enemy state. For instance, if the source was recruited at a petroleum industry business conference, the source may be asked to cozy up to businessmen and women from the enemy state-owned oil corporation and hope to get on to professional message boards or in chat rooms with those individuals and report back routinely with information.

Cyber Reconnaissance Example

Using cyber domain-enabled HUMINT to better operational capabilities through cyber reconnaissance is a bit less straightforward than the other examples. To get information that would lead to easier exploitation and access of the state-owned oil corporation, you could make fake job postings in information technology fields that were very appealing to get as many candidates as possible but with the specific goal of finding applicants who currently or previously worked at the state-owned oil corporation. In interviewing these applicants, you would be looking to get information from them regarding technologies they worked on at the oil corporation or other information relevant to the targeting of cyber domain systems of interest.

Physical-Cyber Example

Since we addressed the aspects of cyber-physical operations in the cyber-attack chapter, I thought it would be interesting to represent the opposite type of operation regarding intelligence gathering. Cyber-physical actions are those where execution of an activity in the cyber domain has tangible effects in another warfighting domain such as air, land, sea, or space. Conversely, physical-cyber operations are those where activity in the physical domains enables effects or activities in the cyber domain. An example of this that falls within the human source collection methodology involves leveraging an asset to perform an action with something physical, such as installing a piece of software that logs keystrokes on devices, he or she has physical access to. If an asset was tasked with installing such software in an internet café they frequented and that software logged what was typed on the installed computers and sent the data back to the collecting party, this would be an example of a physical-cyber human-sourced collection activity.

Direct Collection

To reiterate, direct collection is the act of taking data from a target system in the cyber domain. That data may be from any of the six intelligence collection disciplines (SIGINT, OSINT, HUMINT, MASINT, IMINT, and GEOINT) due to the nature of data that can be found during cyber intelligence collection.

Non-cyber Example

A non-cyber-directed intelligence collection effort would be having an agent sneak into the oil corporation headquarters after hours, breaking into the executive offices and taking pictures or making copies of (both technically IMINT) sensitive information that will be passed along for analysis. Since human beings have competed with each other for resources, direct intelligence collection was actually primarily done through means of HUMINT, though with the advent of the computer age and imagery satellites that has certainly changed. As such another good example of non-cyber direct collection is in fact imagery aircraft and later imagery satellites that circle the Earth taking pictures (IMINT) of areas of interest. Technically in modern day, this would be considered OSINT, but in times such as the cold war where satellite photography was not well known, and spy planes were shot at when entering enemy airspace, it was certainly not open source.

Cyber Intelligence Example

An example of direct cyber intelligence collection would be using a cyber tool to collect emails from important individuals off of an enemy state server. These emails could include any information and are not likely all of intelligence value (cat pictures). That doesn't mean that they won't sometimes contain overly sensitive and valuable information that they aren't supposed to. Collection of enemy state emails might focus on when oil sales are made. Such efforts might also be against military or government email servers to collect anything from future plans to troop movements and supply statuses.

Cyber Reconnaissance Example

This is probably the most appropriate example and easiest to understand of all. Efforts of direct cyber reconnaissance to further cyber domain missions involve any sort of scanning or target enumeration to identify vulnerabilities on a target system or in a target network. Cyber reconnaissance is not always this straightforward though and can be quite complex. Instead of looking for intelligence on an email server like the proceeding example, we could only focus on the email accounts of known IT and administration personnel. This is done in hopes of coming across an email with passwords or other target system information that could further enable access to the enemy state attack surface.

Physical-Cyber Example

A physical enabled example of direct intelligence collection within the cyber domain could be as simple as having someone plug in a thumb drive to computers at a business conference where the enemy state oil corporation was represented. A tool on the thumb drive would infect the machines it was plugged in with a backdoor that allowed cyber actors to access the enemy system for further actions such as intelligence gathering. This type of physical-cyber activity is particularly effective when systems are not available to access in some way from the internet due to not living on any sort of network connected to any other networks. In this case, physical-cyber efforts may be the only way to access those target systems.

Indirect Collection

Indirect collection is the act of gathering information about a target cyber system and not from that cyber system. The information collected this way is often referred to as metadata.

Non-cyber Example

Indirect collection against the enemy state could involve using imagery from a satellite taken routinely over the main port used by the enemy oil corporation. These photographs would reveal the tankers as they come and go. This imagery might allow the gathering party to identify how much oil is in the ships by how low they are sitting in the water. The direction of their travel and flags they are sailing under might tell the gathering party who is buying the oil. Both of these pieces of information would prove valuable in an effort to analyze the compliance with sanctions of involved parties.

Cyber Intelligence Example

Indirect cyber intelligence can be gathered in many ways but often focuses on communication relationships. This means a focus on who is talking to who, for how long, when, and from where. This stays indirect if it is only a collection of metadata and not the actual content of those conversations. Exploitation of an enemy state email server or cellular phone database allows for this type of data to be collected. It may seem invaluable to not get the actual conversations, but this type of collection does lend itself better to data analytics which could lead to more appropriate targeting for direct collection. Further, files of conversations, if they even existed, would likely be much larger than just aggregating the metadata of conversation relationships, and it is probably more efficient than an effort to go through than listening or reading a bunch of conversations.

Cyber Reconnaissance Example

Indirect cyber reconnaissance focuses on the same attributes of communications, who talks to who, for how long, in what manner, and when. This time though, the focus might be on gathering a baseline for how systems on a target network communicate over the course of weeks. With this information in hand, further activity in that target network can be tailored to blend in more with the expected traffic and lower the risk of detection.

This would allow cyber domain operations to potentially continue more efficiently and unimpeded in the cyberspace of the enemy state.

Physical-Cyber Example

What if we needed to know the metadata on phone conversations in an enemy state but we didn't know where to find or how to access the digital databases in the cyber realm that had that information. We could leverage physical access to cell towers on the border with the enemy state and have an actor physically attach hardware to a few of the cell towers that would record this metadata for us and send it out over cellular communications to be collected. This is obviously not as stealthy as doing it entirely within the cyber domain, but it could be the only option.

Understanding the Trade-Off

The most important take away from this chapter and the two that proceeded it is that there exists both interdependencies and trade-offs when making the decision to conduct a cyber-attack. Where exploitation and its enabled intelligence collection may go years without being detected, if ever, cyber-attacks immediately bring attention to the attacker presence within the enemy cyberspace. The technical ramifications posed by the relationships between exploitation, attack, and intelligence gathering will be covered in depth in a later chapter. At the non-technical level, there is the simple concepts of being noticed and being attributed, an enemy that successfully does both has caught the perpetrating entity, and whether intended as an act of war or not, that activity may be considered by the target state as cyber warfare and directly lead to declared and open conflict.

It all comes down to a cost-benefit analysis of the situation. Is it worth losing potentially years of future collection opportunity in a target network to conduct a single cyber-attack? There is no one answer; it depends on the value of the intelligence and the value of the attack. Is it better to eliminate a single capability being developed by an enemy or is it worth being able to monitor the capabilities they develop over the course of an entire conflict or longer? Is it worth shutting off power via malware deployed to power stations in certain areas to hinder the enemy or is it more important to be able to keep the power on and track their movement and actions using exploited state digital surveillance devices? A cyber-attack may save the life of a covert asset in the enemy state by deleting camera recordings, but intelligence gathering over the course of years from that same camera may have prevented the loss of countless lives by providing information that stopped several terrorist attacks.

The weight and authority of such decisions is why cyber-attack falls under Title 10 authority and military command and the applicable oversight to those actions. Though it may not initially have sounded like a very military domain of warfighting, hopefully now the cyber domain can be seen as equally requiring the same doctrine needed when making command decisions that may lead to the loss of some lives in the protection of the many.

Summary

In this chapter we covered the topic of intelligence gathering, how it is defined, and how it relates to and within the cyber domain. We covered multiple examples to gain an understanding of how intelligence gathering within the cyber domain falls into the four collection categories of open source, human source, direct, and indirect. The difference between cyber intelligence gathering and cyber reconnaissance was also discussed and shown through examples. Lastly, the impact of cyber-attack activities to intelligence gathering efforts was highlighted as a matter of extreme importance and a likely motivation for placing attack effects in the cyber domain under the charge of warfighting commanders and the authority of the Department of Defense.

CHAPTER 6

Enemy Attribution

Attribution in the cyber sense is the act of tying together cyber activities based on their attributes to determine that they are coming from the same actor. To make this a relevant effort in cyber warfare, we must take attribution a step further if possible and identify the actual entity the attributed actor represents. If you think about all the authority and legality required to wage cyber warfare, it could not realistically be done unless attribution is taken to its full conclusion and an actual enemy is identified. Even then, just because an enemy has been identified does not mean the action attributed to that enemy is an act of war. A graphical representation of the attribution process is shown in Figure 6-1.

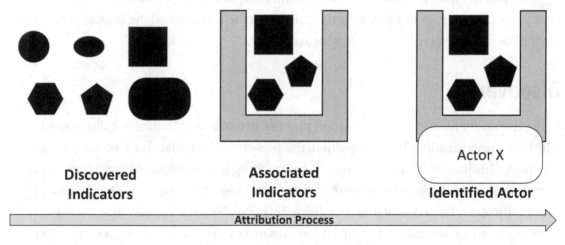

Figure 6-1. *Logical Attribution*

The greatest challenge in identifying and responding to acts of war within the cyber domain is the extreme difficulty in determining the motive of that enemy activity. In fact, unless that activity is indisputably a cyber-attack effect, it cannot responsibly be considered an act of war regardless of who it is attributed to. Further, this chapter will

© Jacob G. Oakley 2019
J. G. Oakley, *Waging Cyber War*, https://doi.org/10.1007/978-1-4842-4950-5_6

reveal that even when cyber activity is positively a cyber-attack, unless the perpetrator outright declares themselves as the actor, attribution and identification of an enemy is unlikely. It is nearly impossible to attribute and identify with high enough fidelity that a declaration of war or warfighting responses within Title 10 authorities would be appropriate.

Logical Process of Attribution

Cyber attribution at a very high level is essentially a four-part process consisting of the following steps:

1. Discovering indicators of compromise

2. Associating them together as belonging to specific actors based on their attributes

3. Identification of the actor

4. Determining the motive of the actor

The vast complexity involved in the technical aspects of attribution will be covered in later parts of this chapter, but it is initially necessary to understand the logical process of attribution as well as why attribution is carried out.

Discovery

In the discovery phase of the attribution process, artifacts and indicators, discovered within the organization that may point to the presence of an unauthorized activity, are identified. Indicators of compromise can be anything from obviously illegitimate actions or even suspiciously timed legitimate activity, and in building the complete picture of these indicators, both digital evidence from the cyber domain and physical clues must be considered as possible indicators. As such, sources that identify artifacts and other indicators of compromise can be as diverse as a user noticing their machine is running slower than normal, a person within the organization acting abnormal, or a piece of security software showing an alert. To illustrate how challenging, it can be at times to decipher if an occurrence is an indicator of compromise, imagine that for over a week the security systems across an organization had not a single alert. This too can be an indicator of compromise, especially if most weeks there are at least several alerts of one kind or another. In this example perhaps a malicious actor changed settings on security systems or manipulated their ability to detect activities they normally would.

Association

Association might be the most integral portion of the attribution process. I say this because if association is done incorrectly, it can make identification and discerning a motivation impossible or wildly inaccurate. Association is simply the grouping together of discovered indicators based on one or more attributes. Here, the great challenge is knowing what to associate and what not to associate. Imagine you have 100 indicators discovered within your organization. We simply went off the attribute of the organization targeted we could falsely interpret that all 100 indicators were associated with a singular actor. Similarly, all 100 indicators probably each have at least one attribute that sets them apart. This could be used to inaccurately decide that all 100 were from 100 different actors based on the time of occurrence down to the 10th of a second. Real indicators often have many attributes, and some will line up and others won't. It is deciding which are more important, more reliable, and more likely to tie together indicators to a specific actor within the organization that drives good association of indicators into the picture of a unique actor and its actions.

Identification

With a set of indicators sufficiently tied to one actor within the organization, it is necessary to identify the likely culprit behind that activity. Some attributes of indicators can lend themselves to identifying potential actors whom are sources of the malicious activity. As an example, if the activity only ever occurs between certain hours, which aren't normal business hours of the target organization, perhaps that reflects a normal work day for the perpetrator. Oftentimes one of the best identifying attributes for who the attacker might be is simply who the target is. Take, for instance, an attack on Indian government computers, even without identifying the remote source of the activity, one potentially leading candidate for malicious activity might be Pakistan simply based off the hostile relationship between the two countries. Identification takes as much finesse as appropriate association does and involves digital evidence, judgment, as well as intelligence and situational awareness of who may benefit from the type of activity tied to the actor.

Motivation

Motivation is most important when considering a response to cyber domain activities, and it also requires satisfactory completion of the first three steps of attribution. The process of attribution is a series of information sets and deductions that build on each other to create the story of a compromise. This story represents what was done in the organization, how many unique actors were doing it, who those actors are, and why they were performing that activity. No matter how many indicators of compromise are found within an organization and how well they are grouped into relating to different actors, response requires more. To respond to a cyber domain activity, the perpetrator needs to be known with a high level of certainty and the motivation clearly understood if we hope to decide on what response the activity justifies, if any. Figure 6-2 shows the attribution process carried out to the point of identifying motivation.

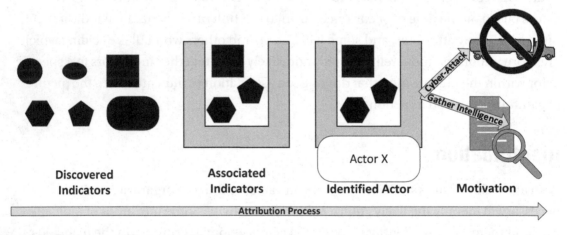

Figure 6-2. *Complete Attribution*

Post-attribution Process

Complete or partial attribution processes are used to derive what type response should be carried out. It is just as important to consider the completeness of the attribution process as it is to consider how reliably each step was carried out. If we carry out the attribution process to conclusion and have decided on both an identification and motivation, we may still be unable to act on that conclusion if the level of confidence is not high enough. On the other hand, if we are only able to perform association and can get no further in the process but have an extremely high level of confidence in our grouping of indicators with a specific actor, it can still lead to very specific response actions. Though this type of response may not be targeted without identification, it can still be just as important to the security of the target of malicious activity. This is especially the case when we consider state actions based on cyber domain activity and its ability to be attributed.

Is Active Response Itself Appropriate?

In a previous chapter, we discussed at length the trade-off between deciding to perform a cyber-attack or if it is perhaps more beneficial to continue to carry out intelligence gathering activities on a given target. This same consideration needs to be levied against any decision we base on attribution. In fact, when attribution results in identification and especially if motivation is determined, it might be wiser to not respond on that information. If an actor is determined to be within an organization, it can be more useful to continue to learn more about what the actor is doing and monitor their activity than kick them out, respond to their actions, or even publicly acknowledge their identity and activity within the network. As far as activity within the cyber domain goes, this non-response could be due to political implications or other non-technical, non-warfighting, or security reasons.

Active Responses

The decision on what to do based on the results of the attribution process are important, and they are more based on the motivation of the actor than its identification or indicator attributes. It is probably accurate to say that even a passive response still represents a reaction to discovered activity. Active responses do require an attributable identification and motivation, and thus, any attribution process that doesn't reliably produce answers to these two phases cannot lead to an active response.

Attack Responses

Active response is extremely important and is fundamental in waging war in the cyber domain. To engage in active cyber domain responses though, the motivation of the actor within the organization or state must be known to be a cyber-attack. Beyond that, the identification of the perpetrator must also be completely known, if not openly acknowledged to lead to an active response. The attribution process is invaluable to this

75

situation where without identity and motivation we cannot know who our enemy is nor how to target them with a response. More than simply driving the active attack response we imagine in warfighting within the cyber domain, identification and motivation can allow the victim state to understand at least a part of the attack methodology and goal of their attacker and thus take actions to better defend themselves.

Non-attack Responses

Non-attack responses are appropriate for any incomplete attribution process, any completed attribution process that identifies motivation of the actor as battlefield preparation or intelligence gathering activity. In all of these examples, the response of the victim state should be to take all possible benefits from the understanding provided by the attribution process and apply it to the security apparatus to improve the state's security posture within the cyber domain. If attribution allows for successful association of indicators into one or more specific actors within the organization, cyber defense activities can be conducted which address threat-specific cyber activities. Where association is unreliable, but indicators and artifacts of compromise activity are found, cyber security activities should be conducted or improved with whatever information is available as cyber security activities are not threat specific but are specific to the victim organization or state. Figure 6-3 identifies potential response actions to attributed actions once motivation is known.

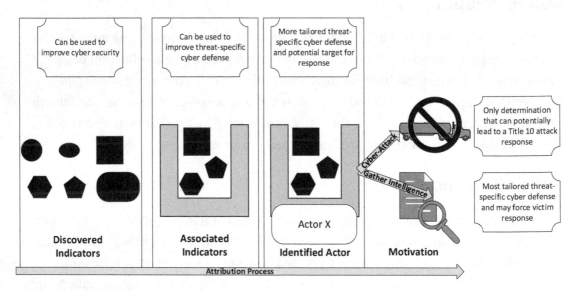

Figure 6-3. *Responses*

Attributes

The attributes of artifacts and indicators of compromise are innumerable in their diversity, so instead of trying to cover them all, we will discuss those that I think are more specific to malicious activity than anything else. The following are also some of the most appropriate attributes that should be used to tie discovered evidence to a specific actor. The attributes we will cover fall into the two broad categories of technical and tactical characteristics.

Technical Attributes

Technical attributes are those which characterize an indicator of compromise or artifact wholly within the cyber domain. The following are several important attributes likely to be associated with discovered evidence of unauthorized activity in a network or organization.

Exploit Tools

Now that you have an understanding of what is meant by exploitation within the cyber domain, I will elaborate a bit further into the technical aspects involved in exploitation to show some of the characteristics different exploit tools might have that can be used to tie them to, or differentiate them from, a known actor. Exploit tools are those weaponized vulnerabilities leveraged to manipulate a target system in an unauthorized way as well as the frameworks and tools that allow hackers to leverage them. By this I mean that a weaponized vulnerability is an exploit tool as is a framework which enables the throwing of such exploits, such as Metasploit or Cobalt Strike. Exploit tools used by the same actor may have many different markers which tie them together or with other types of attributes, but a list of some example exploit tool attributes in the following text might be used to determine whether or not discovered activity belongs to one actor or another.

Exploit tools have many technical characteristics and range widely in their likelihood to be specific to an actor. The vulnerability being leveraged, for instance, if it is a well-known remote code vulnerability, or even something like a misconfiguration, it is difficult to tie exploit tools together as one actor based just on that information. Well-known vulnerabilities are certainly weaponized by many actors, and misconfigurations can be leveraged by anyone who discovered them, so that would be an example of a potentially flawed characteristic to associate exploit tools on. On the other hand, if the vulnerability leveraged is completely unknown (also called a zero-day vulnerability) or it is leveraged in a novel way (zero-day exploit), it is likely a great way of attributing to a single actor.

Frameworks which through exploits can be good for identifying a signature to one actor or another. If multiple different remote code exploits have been discovered within the organization and all are using the same type of communication methodology, it might be a good way to tie to a specific actor. However, if the communication methodology always uses port 4444 for return calls from exploit payloads, and some quick open source research leads us to see that it is a default port for Metasploit. Being a free, publicly available exploit framework, basing actor attribution just on this could be folly as many different attackers (albeit less sophisticated ones) are liable to use this tool and forget or not care to change its default port from 4444.

Access Tools

Access tools are also known as backdoors, remote access tool kits (RATs), and implants, among other monikers. They all have a goal of retaining access to a given system. When used in preparation of a battlefield, this access is being maintained to return and deliver some attack effect at a later time. When being used for intelligence gathering, access tools are used to return to victim systems and continue to gather up-to-date information. In either case access tools often also enable attackers to come back to the installed device at will and use it to pivot deeper within organizations.

Of the many characteristics access tools may have, a subset of them likely to be considered for attribution purposes are the persistence mechanism and binary signatures such as its hash. Persistence, if present, is the way an access tool is set up to maintain its access to a system after reboot or even sometimes after systems are whipped and reinstalled. Just like the exploit tool characteristics, there are good and bad ways to use these attributes. For example, one way of persisting an access tool on a target system is using the built-in scheduler for that operating system. Whether using the "at" or "schtasks" commands on Windows or cron-type functionality on Linux, schedulers have been available in operating systems for decades and can be used for administrative and nefarious reasons all the same. Tying indicators together just because the scheduler of the system was used to re-execute the access tool every time the machine restarted is not a very good way of attributing them to an actor as this type of persistence is easily leveraged by any actor who has exploited or otherwise gained access to the system. If the access tool is persisted in a novel way or an extremely discrete and rarely seen technical fashion, it is likely a great way to associate access tools with a similar actor.

The access tool itself poses a potential attributable characteristic. If the access tool is discovered and sent off to one of many security vendors with signature databases and it comes back as Meterpreter, it is not a good differentiator. This is the default remote access toolkit that ships with the same Kali Linux operating system as the Metasploit exploit framework and for the same reasons could be used by any attacker. If the tool is extremely complex in its functionally, attempts to do something like delete itself upon investigation or simply comes back as never having been seen before based on its size name or other characteristics, it could be a good differentiator between one actor and others.

Attack Effects

Attack effects are interesting to consider for attributable characteristics. Here we essentially get to know the motivation of the attacker before finishing the process of attribution if the effect is obviously used for cyber-attack intent. That being said, it does not mean the perpetrator is attempting to wage cyber war just because there is an attack effect involved. I would like to reference the earlier example of Iranian hackers encrypting systems and demanding ransom to unlock them. Certainly, encrypting whole devices could be considered a cyber-attack especially if the victim device is a military or government system. Attributing an actor and then declaring war against that actor based on an attack effect like this would be similar to declaring war on Canada because some disgruntled hockey fans on the Canadian side of the border are throwing rocks at some US hockey fans on the US side and they accidently hit a border patrol vehicle.

If an attack effect like encrypting or simply deleting a target file system is not a very unique way of attacking a cyber target, it is not a great way to tie actions to an actor. Similarly, if the attack effect doesn't contextually seem like it is likely to be a warfighting action, it is likely safe to assume that the perpetrator was not a warfighter acting on behalf of an enemy state. In such an example, even if attribution was complete, declaration of war is not necessarily the appropriate response as the question of state sponsorship is unanswered or not applicable. If the attack effect is complex, extremely specific, or obviously related to warfighting, it is a good indicator of compromise and probably requires active response if successfully attributed. An attack that encrypts hard drives and happens to effect military computers should not be considered a warfighting action, whereas an attack that takes over control of computers specific to military radar control systems is specific enough in its nature to tie to a unique actor and appropriate to consider active responses.

Redirection Points

I think redirection points are a great way of tying actions to a singular actor, but they are also terrible for use in identification and determining motivation phases of the attribution process. Redirection points are the locations of listening posts or pivot points where traffic from an access tool or exploit tool communicates to and/or from. These are great pieces of information to tie cyber domain activity together because they are tying traffic flows to a source, and that sort of communication channel is extremely unlikely to belong to multiple actors. This could be a location external to the organization, where the initial access tools are beaconing back to. If you, say, discovered one infected system talking out to a random address in Estonia and then you searched your network for logs of traffic talking to the same address, it is very likely those belong to the same actor. Similarly, within the network if you find an access tool communicating back to a specific user machine on a routine basis, and you search your network logs for that sort of communication and you find multiple other machines have been accessed and/or exploited from it, that would be a great attribute to tie actions together with. The actor probably gained access to the user device using malicious email phishing and then used it as a launch point to get deeper into the organization.

The reason redirection points are terrible to use in the identification of an actor or understanding motivation is due to their availability. I could go on any number of cloud hosting services such as Amazon's AWS and, for free, turn on a server based in any number of countries across the world. If I used that server as the home base for my access tools, it isn't really indicative at all of where I am physically sitting or what state is sponsoring my activity. In fact, if as an organization, state, or simply network you see that a tremendous amount of traffic is hitting your firewall from one location or another, it is probably more appropriate to wonder why attackers are using that location to redirect from than to wonder why that location's people are attacking you.

Time

As far as technical attributes go, time is being considered for its association among discovered indicators and artifacts. We will also discuss the tactically applicable indicator of time as well in a later section. When available as a discovered indicator, the attribute of time can be valuable on systems. If you had an alert caused by a security software that said it stopped unauthorized activity, and you then searched your system for events within a few minutes of that time, it might lead you to other suspicious activities. As you find more activities and expand the time window you search in, it may reveal a whole host of indicators that are tied to the activity of a singular actor on the system.

Obviously, time can't be the only tie-in, as systems are often very busy and have many events logged. However, if the alert was only a second later than an error event that referenced a file which was only introduced to the system a minute earlier, and logs show a user authenticated from a remote system and moved it to yours, it's fair to say they are probably the same actor's story of actions on your system. In this way time stamps can be used to both discover additional related activity and tie them to the same actor. Much like the redirection point attribute though, time is mostly useful for tying activities together based on proximity of time stamps to each other.

Tactical Attributes

Tactical attributes are those which while discovered through activity within the cyber domain actually apply more to the actual individuals carrying out that activity.

Timing

We will pick up right where we left off by referencing timing again. Technically speaking we were considering the attribute of time stamping of system events as a way to characterize and activity as belonging to an actor. Tactically speaking we would focus more on the window of time. This attribute is best used when evaluating a large set of indicators across long periods of discovery. Over the course of weeks or even months if cyber domain activity was identified within an organization but fidelity of the attributes was not enough to associate them as a singular actor, timing of operations can be used to do so. Say, for instance, activity over the past months only occurred between 2 PM local and 10 PM local and for seemingly no reason. It could be that 2 PM and 10 PM local for the victim were something like 9 AM and 5 PM local to the actor. Seemingly disparate indicators of compromise that continue to happen over long periods of time and within the same period of time we will consider to be an operational window can allow for those activities to be grouped together.

Targets

As mentioned earlier in this chapter, the target itself can be an indicator if activities belong to the same cyber domain actor. Leveraging this characteristic of an indicator is also extremely fidelity constrained. Take the US military for instance; targeting of the US military by a cyber domain activity could probably be associated with well over 100 other nation states, not to mention actors independent of state-sponsored motivations. Even a specific base or service or unit is probably not enough to reliably use as a tying attribute to associate activities with an actor. At this level of fidelity, the target can certainly narrow down activities to actors from a smaller subset of possibilities.

For instance, if the target of a cyber activity was US PACOM (Pacific Command), we might say that likely actors would be from Asian countries aggressive to the United States such as China or North Korea. I stress that such target fidelity should only be used to narrow down between actors or as a supporting characterization for attribution. If the target was a specific commander or government agent, say, commander of the US forces in South Korea, or ambassador to South Korea, it becomes a bit safer to rely on such indicators as attributing to specific actors and even their identities. Another interesting way of leveraging indicators of compromise to identify perpetrators is in widespread activities.

Many security companies who do reports of large attack activities map out the number of infected hosts by country. If an attack had, say, 90% of its affected end points in areas of countries with Kurdish populations, it might be understandably deductive to associate that activity with a country who considers the Kurds a threat, such as Turkey. This type of characteristic used in this way also can cast a wider net of possibilities. Say a cyber activity has many different countries infected, but over 90% are all within a country like Russia. Since many countries probably have espionage and intelligence gathering efforts against Russia, it might narrow down the perpetrator identity to a subset of state sponsorships, but it would still be a large pool of potential actors and therefore not necessarily great for attribution.

Sophistication

Sophistication is a tricky characteristic to utilize as it requires much technical understanding of offensive cyber operations within the cyber domain as well as how enemies are likely to target your organization. This difficulty though does not impact its value when correctly applied in analysis of indicators and artifacts. There are several sophistication-specific attributes we would look to discern about various indicators when using sophistication markers to tie activities together and to actors.

First there is sophistication of the attack indicated. This is not a technical characteristic but a tradecraft one. Regardless of whether the attack used advanced and complex tools or open source and readily available operating system functionalities to accomplish compromise, we are looking at the strategy of the attack. Well-known tools and techniques can be used but combined in extremely creative and effective ways to achieve compromise goals in the cyber domain. If indicators and artifacts gathered over the course of months or years point to an extremely creative and adaptable adversary that might allow for tying seemingly diverse technical capabilities together as being from one specific actor.

Conversely, very advanced tools can be used in very simplistic efforts and also indicate a unique and specific actor was involved. Recently, more than one advanced and technically sophisticated exploitation tools have been leaked on the internet and seemingly were created with state sponsorship simply based on the effort involved in their inherent sophistication. Those tools and exploits have then been used in all manner of attacks by amateur hackers and professional criminals alike. In this situation the advanced sophistication that was involved in the technical aspects of the tool were not indicative of a unique actor, but the blunt application of the sophisticated tool might be.

The last facet of sophistication in cyber activity I would like to point out for inclusion in attribution efforts is that of conscious attempts to avoid attribution. This is the hallmark of an advanced threat, and the method of detection avoidance and the regularity of it can certainly pair with other characteristics of indicators to associate activity with specific actors. This is true of extremely careful actors who clean up after themselves and hide in baseline noise of organizations as well as those who have no care for such efforts. Some adversaries can be attributed by their distinct lack of discipline or even uncaring attitude toward being identified or called out by an attribution process.

Forget Everything You Thought You Knew

We have already covered how both technical and tactical attributes used to associate activity with actors can be within themselves very accurate and frustratingly unreliable. Unfortunately, even with good characterization of technical and tactical attributes used for associated activity, there is a mountain of uncertainty between those data points and a complete and appropriate attribution process. That is because nearly every single artifact or indicator of compromise in the cyber domain can have been altered, fabricated, or even be a false positive, and there is similarly almost no way of detecting if it was tampered with depending on the situation.

I mentioned how the port 4444 on return traffic communicating to an exploit framework was indicative of using Metasploit or Meterpreter. Any attack framework and any exploit payload could also be configured to do the same. An attacker might do this out of chance, picking 4444 not thinking it will associate them with an open source tool. They also may be doing it on purpose to make investigators think they are an amateur hacker and not a state-sponsored intelligence gathering activity within the cyber domain. Access tools might utilize a persistence mechanism known to be associated with a particular well-acknowledged actor. This might be because it was the only thing available to persist the access tool and the actor took a chance it might not get caught. It could also be because the actor is going to conduct a cyber-attack activity and wants to frame the well-acknowledged group to hopefully steer investigations and responses away from itself.

Time stamps on files and in logs can be changed, edited, or deleted in almost every case if the actor has sufficient context on the system via exploitation. This can make activity look benign or simply make it very difficult to associate together or to an actor. Actors could also conduct their operations on the same schedule as typical work days local to the target systems and state, this avoiding connection to their possible location via operational Windows. A nation state could infect machines in its own cyberspace with the same tools used to attack enemy assets. This way if the activity were discovered and the tools signature by antivirus companies, the subsequent reports would show heat maps with potentially even more compromises in the aggressing country than the victim country. That would certainly throw off reliable attribution and make any sort of non-cyber domain warfighting response to a cyber-attack action seem unprovoked and unacceptable.

Lastly much like the port usage making some other tool appear to communicate like the open source Metasploit and Meterpreter, actors could simply leverage those open source tools themselves. Sophistication is only reliable as an attribute if the actor themselves is actively trying to appear less sophisticated than they are capable of to avoid deduction that the activity they are conducting is associated with a nation state.

Unsteady Foundation

Though these recent revelations may make complete attribution seem rather hopeless, there is one way to try and determine how reliable a given indicator or artifact may be. If the sophistication of an attacker is likely known due to some otherwise provided intelligence or a likely identification of the actor perpetrating the activity, we have room for some deduction. Say I know the actor likely targeting me is not one who is very sneaky or careful or cares about being attributed. In this case I can tentatively assume that when I discover indicators and artifacts, it is not likely they were altered, at least not by the actor I assume to be targeting me. All you can essentially do at this point is say whether or not the indicator is likely tied to an uncaring and probable careless actor or it is potentially evidence of a more sophisticated cyber activity.

Aside from the ability of attributes to be altered, and this can impact the attribution process, there is also a concept of reliability and fidelity to attributes in general. For each attribute used to create an actor profile or potentially characteristics that tie indicators together and to actors, there must be other considerations as well.

I can think of one great example for this. Imagine you discover some activity within your organization, and you tie much of it to a singular actor who has been using a well-known vulnerability and exploit incorporated into an open source exploitation framework. You should have already patched or removed vulnerable systems, but it just wasn't a huge priority and the portion of the organization these activities were found in were not of much consequence, so you assume it is some amateur hacker and not likely a state-sponsored activity that warrants more dire responses. However, upon further attempts at correlating indicators of compromise and artifacts within your network, you realize that the same access tool installed after the exploit was used on the initially discovered machines is actually present on many systems in more crucial and sensitive areas of the organization. Upon investigating those systems, you determine that the access tool has been present on them for over 5 years and that the same exploit was used to gain access. You look at the information online for the well-known exploit and vulnerability and read that it was only publicly known starting 4 years ago. Now the picture is much different; now it seems you were the target of likely state-sponsored cyber activities which leveraged at the time, zero-day exploits; and worse, this actor has been active in your network over the course of half a decade.

Summary

In this chapter we covered the logical process of attribution involved in cyber domain activities and their perpetrating actors. We discussed the different types of responses to attributed activity and the level of attribution required to justify them. We covered characteristics of indicators of compromise and artifacts that are indicative of malicious cyber activities. We covered where they were both appropriate and inappropriate at associating activities with actors as well as how easily they were altered.

The goal of this chapter was to educate the reader on just how unrealistic it is to expect the attribution process to end with identification of the actor and an understanding of motivation. This is not even considering that most compromises go unnoticed for months or years, and even if attribution was complete, it is probably not timely. Given these now known factors in cyber warfare, you should understand that timely active response to cyber activity is an irresponsible expectation and action. Even if a cyber domain activity led to a cyber-attack effect that was immediately detected, the attribution process would not allow for anything resembling a real-time return of fire which is what the warfighter expects and has learned to rely on. We must therefore accept both the lack of appropriateness in the return fire concept within cyber warfare and its inherent technical and tactical difficulties. Essentially, short of an activity being positively admitted as a cyber-attack effect openly acknowledged by a state government as a warfighting action, there won't be responsible or reliable recompense. Attempting to perform return fire activities within cyber, land, air, sea, or space domains without this type of open acknowledgment is a fool's errand and likely to be interpreted by outside observers as unprovoked and reckless. As such, it would violate some if not all of the previously discussed political and legal constraints to waging a cyber war.

CHAPTER 7

Targeting

Successful completion of the attribution process is done via a positive identification of the perpetrating actor and infallible determination of that actor's motivation. If that motivation is deemed to be a cyber-attack, by open acknowledgment of irrefutable proof, we have established that we have an enemy. This enemy is one that is engaged in warfighting activity, targeting us, within the cyber domain. At this point that enemy must be considered as being openly engaged in conflict with our own state. As such, responses to the enemy state's cyber-attack could be from or within any combination of warfighting domains. It might be appropriate to ignore, sanction, respond in kind, or escalate to something such as a kinetic capability like a missile or bomb. For the purposes of this book, we will not attempt to weigh out appropriate non-cyber responses to cyber-attacks of enemy states. Instead I will outline how a cyber response action could actually be conceived and executed.

Most importantly to cyber activity as a warfighting construct is an understanding of how the enemy and the actual target of a response action differ. The enemy identified by the attribution process may not be a specific actor but the wider state behind that actor. This is why motivation, and specifically a Title 10–like attack motivation, must be determined to drive a similar response. In a Title 10–like activity, the attribution process may determine a specific unit, organization, or even individual behind cyber activity. However, since it is Title 10–type activity, it is attributed to the sponsoring state, as the individual, unit, or organization is considered an agent of that state. Also, in this case, the attributed state is now considered an enemy, and there is a potential for open conflict or even declared war with that enemy.

© Jacob G. Oakley 2019
J. G. Oakley, *Waging Cyber War*, https://doi.org/10.1007/978-1-4842-4950-5_7

Tactical vs. Strategic Response

Attribution resulting from Title 10 cyber activity could establish a foreign state as an enemy in a declared conflict. In response to that specific Title 10 activity which initiated the conflict itself, the victim state is likely to conduct its own warfighting activity. Such a response may target the enemy state-sponsored perpetrating unit, or it might be something else.

Think of the bombing of Pearl Harbor. That action led to open and declared war between the United States and the Empire of Japan. The first real response by the United States didn't target the Japanese naval fleet which launched the attack on Pearl Harbor. Instead the US government and military felt it more strategically appropriate to respond by attacking the Japanese homeland. This was accomplished by the Doolittle Raid, an attack by US bombers launched from naval vessels which dropped ordinance on the Japanese capital of Tokyo and other locations on the island of Honshu. This was done to send a message that the United States could also strike far across the Pacific Ocean at the Japanese home front. In this example the enemy was determined to be the Empire of Japan, and the target of the response was determined to be Tokyo, not the warfighters responsible for the attack on Pearl Harbor. At a tactical level, US forces attempted to return fire and ward off parts of the attack during the air raid over Hawaii. This return fire was a tactical response to an ongoing attack and not a strategic response as part of a larger conflict like the Doolittle Raid was.

The attack on Pearl Harbor is a great analogy for describing some of the constraints and challenges to cyber warfare. In cyber warfare, it would be hard to know that there was enemy activity against victim assets until the actual attack happens. Also, in the cyber domain, the tool that launched the attack effect may have been put in place months or years earlier. It is very likely that when the enemy has launched their attack they have been gone for a long while or at least are in the process of moving on to other targets. In cyber warfare, the attack effect is logically the last action an enemy actor will take within a network or organization. After the attack is launched, victim systems may be no longer accessible due to the type of attack. Additionally, the victim network is now aware that an actor has been within it and is probably on high alert and far more likely to thwart further Title 10– or even Title 50–type activities by an enemy within it.

Similarly, the Japanese attack on Pearl Harbor happened after much planning, strategic decision-making, preparation, and a long naval journey to Hawaii. Once the attack was launched, the Japanese fleet involved headed back away from Hawaii. Consider if they had stayed around Hawaii or even decided to attack other parts of the

United States such as California. With hostilities now openly known, their attacks would likely be less effective if not a complete failure. The decision to strike Pearl Harbor was a strategic one by the Japanese Empire, and the attack itself was a tactical mission with its own tactical decisions within it. The only tactical response by the United States would be any exchange of fire between the US forces at Pearl Harbor and the perpetrating actors. Outside of actively engaging the attacking force during the attack, the response by the United States was decided at the strategic level as part of the wider conflict.

In fact, the US response didn't take place until April 12, 1942, over 4 months after the December 7, 1941, attack on Pearl Harbor and the declaration of war by the United States on December 8, 1941. Though the open conflict was addressed by the United States the next day with a declaration of war, careful planning and consideration went into the strategic decision of how to respond to this new enemy and which enemy target and attack effect was appropriate. Imagine if the US response was as immediate as the declaration of war. The closest naval and air resources to Hawaii were probably days away at minimum. Also, any attempt to find the Japanese forces in the wide expanse of the Pacific Ocean, before the age of jet aircraft and imagery satellite, would like have proved futile so any attempt at a direct response to the perpetrating agent of the Japanese Empire was out of consideration.

Cyber warfare requires the same tactful response considerations. There is not a possibility for tactical response to ongoing actions such as a return of fire to the perpetrating unit. This is because the enemy is not actually present at the target being attacked, they are anywhere in the world with an internet connection, if there is a human involved at all. The attack is also potentially a leave-behind set to go off at some triggered event and not an active action by a human, even if a cyber return fire capability existed, it would have no effect. This is not to say that as part of open conflict, cyber-attack effects won't target enemy cyber warfighting assets or capabilities. Simply put, any decision to conduct cyber warfare against an enemy is decided at the strategic level and not the tactical one. Warfighting responses from the cyber domain are not technically nor tactically possible as a return fire action to an ongoing enemy attack. This is extremely important to understand as we move forward with our discussion on how targeting decisions for cyber warfighting effects are made.

Let's revisit the Pearl Harbor analogy one last time. Imagine that the naval ships docked in Pearl Harbor as well as the Japanese aircraft carriers and aircraft were all remotely piloted like modern-day drones. For this example, let's also say that the Japanese planes dropped one load of bombs and then left US airspace immediately to return to their aircraft carriers which then steamed homeward and the United States had no anti-aircraft capabilities in Pearl Harbor. The attack would be launched, US assets would be destroyed, but there would be no active engagement between the US ships and the Japanese aircraft or fleet. Realizing what happens, the United States still declares war the next day, but obviously there is no realistic way to go after the Japanese fleet, so they strategically consider how to send a similar message what the Japanese just did, which is the Doolittle Raid deep into the Japanese Empire.

A cyber domain Pearl Harbor–like incident would play out the same way. The enemy would execute its attack capability. Let's say the cyber-attack took over the computers driving many US aircraft during the over 100 aircraft JFEX exercise and crashed them all into the ground. Let's also say the enemy state then openly acknowledged the attack. The duration of that attack effect, from the point where the aircraft computers were taken over until they crashed into the ground, would be only minutes. During that attack effect window, there is not time to return fire, nor a target readily identifiable as the attack took place in US airspace, aboard US aircraft which crashed on US soil. Such a cyber-attack effect could have been put in place months even years prior to the exercise. As an example, let's say the cyber-attack tool was introduced to the aircraft systems due to supply chain interdiction 4 years earlier. The aggressor nation swapped legitimate computer chips used for an upgrade of the aircraft computer systems with one of their own malicious design mid-shipment. The attack triggered when the planes flew over the airspace used for the JFEX exercise over Nevada which is always held in the same place each time and is the biggest air exercise the United States conducts.

This is only a hypothetical scenario which is however it clearly illustrates that any response to a cyber-attack will involve a strategic decision-making process for target selection and attack methodology. One last time, there is no realistic scenario for cyber-attack effect return fire. There is no effective or realistic potential for actively targeting enemy cyber forces during their attack. The victim may respond at a later date by targeting the cyber forces, but it won't happen while their attack is going on. Remember, without positively knowing the intention and motivation of cyber activity, we cannot realistically determine if it is Title 10–type actions or Title 50. The cyber activity that prepared the battlefield for the effect by installing the attack tool took place years earlier. Even if the actor was caught during their supply chain interdiction attempt, there is no way of easily determining what the malicious chips actually did. Even if we did reverse engineer them and determine they could crash planes, we still can't know if the enemy was going to actually execute the attack effect so we could not launch our own Title

10 activity or declare open hostilities just off catching them during their interdiction operation. Thus, we have elaborated on earlier positions that we cannot determine motivation positively as being Title 10 in nature and respond in kind until the attack is actually executed. Additionally, since the attack was essentially launched years before hand, there is no opportunity to tactically return fire with a cyber-attack of our own.

I feel I have belabored this point with my own opinion and analogous examples enough now. I do so because there is constantly this talk of engaging cyber enemies in military and political circles and that is just not a realistic possibility. As you also now realize, actively engaging cyber adversaries is simply not how cyber warfighting would work. It is in fact far more likely that we were able to respond to an ongoing cyber-attack effect using something kinetic like a missile or bomb. This however is also an extremely unlikely scenario. Now that we have arduously gone over why, we will move forward accepting that any cyber response to an act of war, be it cyber or otherwise, will be deterministically and strategically decided in regard to both target selection and manner of effect. Next, I will cover how we move from knowing who the enemy is to decide what part of that enemy to target and with what kind of attack.

Target Selection

With hostilities declared, the enemy identified, and a cyber response determined to be appropriate, we need to decide what we want to target with a cyber response and what we want that attack effect to be. If we pause to think about that though, it is much more logical that cyber-attack effects are chosen for use based on the target and not vice versa. It makes more sense for a target to be selected first and then cyber warfighting conducted if deemed the appropriate way of affecting that target. Unlike some warfighting options in other domains, such as cruise missiles and nuclear bombs, cyber weapons rely on at least a fundamental understanding of the target to actually work. We don't need to know the inner workings of an enemy troop transport to hit it with a missile and destroy it. If we wanted to use a cyber-attack to instead crash the vehicle or simply kill its engines, we actually need to accomplish several feats. We need to get our attack tool installed on the truck, and with enough privileges that it can take adequate actions to execute the attack activity when called upon.

What we will not attempt to do in this book is identify what type of attack effects are appropriate in response to what aggressions. Those kinds of decisions I will leave to strategists and commanders involved in real conflict. What we will do though is walk through the process of targeting and scoping whatever enemy resource is identified. In offensive cyber security assessments such as penetration testing or red teaming, accurate scoping of those engagements drives the rest of the process and ultimately determines how successful the assessment can be. Cyber-attack targeting is much the same. The scope and method of the attack dictate the entire tactical decision-making process during a cyber-attack mission. Since we have also determined that the targets available to cyber warfighting are limited to those targets for which the aggressor can develop working attack effects, we will focus on that concept first.

Appropriate Targets

Like any other warfighting capability, targets of cyber warfare are largely constrained by feasibility. There are many factors that weigh into the decision to use a cyber weapon. The following list consist of what I believe to be some essential considerations:

1. A cyber-attack effect is the best option available to deny or manipulate the target.

2. A cyber-attack effect already exists that produces the desired denial or manipulation of the target, or

3. A cyber-attack effect that produces the desired denial or manipulation of the target is capable of being developed in a timeline that supports the intended strategic benefit.

4. There is a realistic potential for access of the enemy target and delivery of the cyber-attack effect.

The Cyber Option

What makes a cyber-attack effect the right choice when targeting enemy resources? In the increasingly internetworked world within which war must be fought, cyber is likely to increase in the future as a weapon of choice. It has the benefit of being launched with no inherent danger to the perpetrating agents of the state which is no small thing. Another benefit to cyber over kinetic weapons is that they can be positioned and left behind to be triggered only when deemed necessary. If one country feared aerial invasion by another and was able to compromise their aircraft as discussed in the earlier example, perhaps they would and only intend to trigger the attack effect if the enemy state invades their airspace. There is also the optics of cyber warfare. At least for now, and until someone uses cyber weapons to target something like a hospital or accidentally kills innocents, cyber warfare is perceptively non-violent. This means retribution on the conducting state by the wider international community is less likely, if it could be tied back to that state at all. There are plenty of other reasons to choose a cyber option for Title 10–type attack actions as opposed to something such as an invasion force or cruise missile. Regardless of the reasons, the decision that a cyber-attack is the most appropriate or best-case scenario is the first step in targeting an enemy resource with a cyber warfighting activity.

Existing Capability

If cyber-attack is considered preferential to conventional options, then there must also be an existing attack capability as the development timelines of a new cyber-attack effect would likely make it not a first choice. The capability to attack the enemy resource must be readily available and must produce an effect that realizes the strategic need to attack that resource in the first place. For instance, one state may have a cyber weapon capable of affecting its enemy's tanks. Tanks are highly computerized weapon systems in today's militaries and could be susceptible to cyber-attacks. One cyber weapon may be capable of shutting down the electric engine controls for the tank, stopping it dead in its tracks. Another cyber weapon may be able take over the firing and targeting system of the main canon so that ordinance went off inside the barrel when fired. Both effects are considered cyber-attacks and as such would fall under Title 10 definitions; however, maybe one of those effects delivered the strategic goal of the intended attack and the other did not. If the goal was to take over the enemy tanks for later use, then having the canon discharge into the tank and destroy it would not be strategically viable. Therefore, even if a cyber-attack effect exists, it must deliver the intended impact to be a viable choice.

Developing the Capability

If a capability that meets the strategic impact requirement for targeting an enemy resource does not exist, cyber warfare may still be appropriate if there is a realistic possibility it can be developed. The real consideration in this case is whether or not that development will happen in a time frame which doesn't change the strategic viability of the attack. Say we consider the same two cyber-attacks against tanks we just discussed.

There might be a realistic capability that the non-destructive cyber-attack could be developed, but perhaps it is likely to take 6 months. If the enemy is planning on invading with their tanks in the coming weeks, this would not be an appropriate target selection. Just because it would be best to target an enemy resource with a cyber-attack and there is possibility of finding an attack effect that delivers the needed impact does not mean it is a responsible choice of weapon. Time and other constraints can drastically alter the feasibility of a cyber-attack.

Access to the Target

In some cases, a cyber-attack target may be readily accessible across internet connections from the attacking state to the enemy. In any other case, there must be an ability to access the desired resource to then deliver the attack effect. Imagine the Japanese Empire decided an aerial bombardment of Pearl Harbor the best attack scenario against the United States but that they did not have aircraft carriers. Their planes had nowhere near enough range to make it from any outpost to the Hawaiian Islands and then, despite being the best attack option, aerial bombardment would no longer be within the consideration of attack options. We will discuss the challenges and requirements for developing access in the next chapter, but for targeting decisions, there simply needs to be an existing ability to access the target for delivery of cyber-attack effect tools or a realistic possibility of creating that access.

BDA

Battle damage assessment (BDA) is the evaluation of the effectiveness of a stand-off weapon and the damage it inflicted on a target. Traditionally this practice is applied to long-distance missile strikes or bomb drops where the actual striking of the enemy target is not directly observed. BDA is an extremely important aspect of warfare as it allows for continuous assessment of weapon effectiveness. If a missile consistently comes back with poor BDA because it fails to inflict the anticipated destruction on targets, that information needs to be made available to decision makers. This type of information allows strategic decision-making to evolve over the course of a conflict to allow for more effective targeting of enemy resources with friendly weapon systems.

Cyber warfare, with its extremely dispersed engagement situations, needs BDA whenever possible just as cruise missiles or high-altitude bomb drops. If a cyber-attack effect is deemed appropriate and launched at multiple enemy targets but fails to deliver on the strategic goal of those activities, the decision makers need that information. BDA is not simply important to evaluating whether or not a launched weapon, cyber or kinetic, was effective enough to meet the commander's intent for the attack. There is another aspect to BDA which is important to just war concepts and international conventions such as the Geneva Convention.

If BDA comes back indicating a missile is destroying more than intended or with less precision than expected that is extremely important information to commanders and their strategic decision-making needs. Unnecessary destruction and potential harm to innocents and non-combatants is an ugly side effect of any conflict, and if a weapon cannot reliably avoid such impacts, it should cease to be used or at a minimum employed with different rules of engagements. Cyber weapons are no different. Imagine a virus intended to shut off power to military installations spread beyond them and started shutting off power in hospitals and prisons and other places which endangered the non-combatant population of the enemy state. This would be as strong a reason to alter the use of a cyber weapon as excessive collateral damage would be to a missile.

Unfortunately, unlike kinetic weapons, we cannot fly over the target of a cyber strike and evaluate its effectiveness. In attacks enabled by the cyber domain where the attack is a cyber-physical attack with a result noticeable in another warfighting domain such as air, land, space, or sea, we can still potentially evaluate the results and conduct BDA. On the other hand, I do not know the most correct methodology to conducting BDA in cyber domain attack activities. Rather I am asserting that conducting effective warfare in a just war and following international conventions in the conduct of cyber warfare would in part rely upon BDA capabilities which the cyber domain does not easily accommodate.

Target Fidelity

In the previous chapter, we discussed the attribution process and how certain attributes of cyber-attack effects certainly had a shelf life. When the target of a cyber domain attack is another cyber entity such as a computing system, there is a similar concern with the timeliness of target development and subsequent attack. When a computer system is targeted by a cyber-attack, the confirmation of target identity is likely done via electronic addresses such as IP address or MAC address. Those addresses can be changed at literally any time for any number of reasons. This is particularly the case of systems with internet-facing addresses.

The volatility of such addresses is hard to determine. As such, a remote cyber-attack against an internet-facing enemy system is targeted and sent via its IP address. What if between the decision to go ahead and execute the cyber-attack and the exploit operation that put the cyber-attack tool in place, the remote address changed. At this point there is certainly a chance that the state launched a Title 10 cyber-attack against an electronic address that potentially is being used by a completely different state than when it was originally targeted.

There is also the question of cloud-hosted systems and who they legally belong to. Amazon's cloud service AWS may host systems being used by an enemy military or government. As far as Amazon is concerned, those systems belong to the foreign state. The moral and legal authority of attacking such a system is, as of yet, largely unexplored. Does there need to be special consideration to the fact that, though the systems are owned and operated by a foreign state does the hosting by a separate entity affect the legality of Title 10 activity? Additionally, in these types of cloud-hosted networks, the volatility of system addressing can be extreme. Figure 7-1 shows a cyber-attack against an enemy system hosted in such an environment.

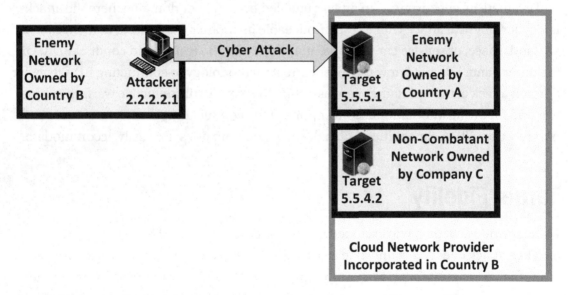

Figure 7-1. *Intended Target*

Figure 7-2 shows what can happen when the lease on public IP addressing changes in a cloud provider between the time the target was decided and the time the attack was executed. The result is a cyber-attack against an inappropriate target, violating international laws and national legal authorities and potentially wasting a cyber-attack capability.

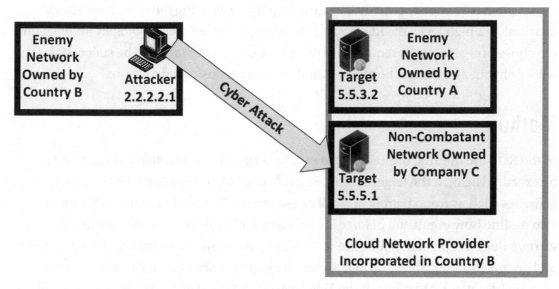

Figure 7-2. *Unintended Target*

Due to the ease with which a target system can appear differently on a network or the internet, target fidelity must be strongly considered and constantly re-evaluated in the target determination process. This is less so the case when an attack tool is installed on the intended target system is simply waiting for the command to execute. In this situation the attack tool may check at certain intervals for an execution command and act only when it is received. In any case the volatility of cyber domain targets specifically must bare increased scrutiny than targets engaged in a cyber-physical nature or via conventional warfare.

Rules of Engagement

The rules of engagement (ROE) for any armed conflict (even one where those arms are exclusively cyber weapons) are largely and generally defined by the national legal authorities of the participating combatants as well as international law and convention as we discussed at the beginning of this book. It is important when conducting cyber warfare to have cyber-specific ROEs pertaining to the carrying out of a cyber-attack mission. At a high level, the ROEs will dictate the permitted methodologies for engaging the chosen target, what is required for the attack against the target to be successful, at what point an attack must be aborted, and when it is considered a failure.

Method

In the ROE the method of attack is laid out. This covers how the attack is intended to be executed against the target system. The role of a ROE differs from other warfighting activities such as troop patrols or naval engagements. In those activities ROEs must also outline how escalation of force is established and executed. As we discussed, cyber warfare does not present return fire or active engagement situations between friendly and enemy forces. Instead the ROE should be strictly defined such that the perpetrator of the cyber-attack can perform the Title 10 activity to deliver the strategically identified target and effect. The ROE also ensures that the allowed actions, if followed correctly, result in a legal and moral act of war. Since the cyber realm shrouds warfighting actions to the point that their intent and actions are easily misinterpreted, there is no room for improper execution of cyber-attack effects.

Success

An ROE should also outline what mission success is. If the mission is to deploy a cyber-attack tool to targets, those conducting that mission need to know when they can stop. This is one way in the cyber domain the ROE limits excessive use of force. It may seem silly in a warfighting domain where bullets and mortars aren't flying around, but it is still extremely important. The strategic decisions that go into deciding on targets and the end effects that are chosen for them are often very complex and situational. Altering the outcome of that mission by an overzealous use of cyber force against enemy systems could impact the outcome to the enemy of the targeted systems suffering the intended attack. Imagine a cyber-attack mission was to cripple 50% of a certain type of systems in an enemy network to get them to react a certain way. If the attack effect is deployed instead to 75% of those systems, the resulting impact to the enemy may dictate they react in a way different than if only half their systems were crippled. If the strategic goal of the mission was not met because an extra 25% of systems were affected, it would not only be an unplanned over-use of force but would negatively impact the strategic efforts that led to the use of cyber-attack effects in the first place.

Abort

Just as a definition of success limits the use of force in cyber warfare to what was intended by strategic decision makers, defining when to abort a mission is just as important. Abort decisions mainly revolve around two issues, a loss of target fidelity and intended attack effect consequences. Loss of target fidelity is essentially what we discussed earlier in this chapter. The decision to abort based on a loss of fidelity prevents the targeting of unintended or potentially innocent systems. If the targeting information leads the attacker to a system which no longer appears to be as it was when the attack was strategically decided, it should be aborted. This avoids negative impact to warfighting strategic goals as well as prevents violations of international convention and national authorities by preventing Title 10 activities from being conducted against improper targets such as non-combatants.

The second aspect involved in cyber-attack mission abort scenarios is any unintended consequences of attack actions. This could be a situation where cyber-attack effects are having unexpected impacts to systems. Imagine 100 enemy systems were potential targets and the mission was to execute the cyber-attack against 50% of them. After the first five attempts, the attack effect is not occurring or perhaps is causing a different effect than was strategically decided as appropriate. This could be because a patch came out for the operating system or other software on the targets which made the attack effect behave in previously unknowable ways. This is certainly a good point to abort an attack mission. There is also the impact attack effects can have on other friendly activities within the cyber domain such as intelligence gathering or battlefield preparations for other missions. Cyber-attacks are likely planned well in advance with careful consideration to how the attack effect will impact things like cyber intelligence gathering activities against the enemy. If the attack effect started behaving unexpectedly for whatever reason, the mission must cease to avoid unintended consequences to other cyber domain activities.

Failure

Though an abort of a cyber mission certainly results in a failure of that mission, there are other reasons that the failure of a mission is decided. Failure of a cyber mission is a result of the cyber-attack effect not being able to achieve the strategic goal within the constraints outlined within the scope of the attack or ROE. For example, let's say that of 100 potential target systems, 50% need to be affected by the cyber-attack within a window of a week. For any number of reasons that may not be possible and at the 1-week mark if 50% have not been exploited, the mission needs to be labeled a failure and a reconvening of the strategic target process conducted. There are any number of mission constraints that if not met could constitute a failure, and in all cases, they are part of what limits cyber-attack effects to appropriate use.

Summary

In this chapter we covered the targeting of enemy resources by cyber-attack effects. We used historical warfighting examples as an instructive analogy for how tactical and strategic decision-making processes are involved in target and effect choices. The reader should walk away with the understanding that actively engaged cyber forces returning fire at each other is an essentially ludicrous and unrealistic scenario in cyber warfare. We then talked about what leads to the decision to use cyber weapons, how to assess their effectiveness with BDAs, as well how target fidelity and ROEs constrain the warfighter in missions within the cyber domain.

CHAPTER 8

Access

With the target determined and the desired end effect decided, the cyber-attack mission is considered scoped. Deciding on the target is only the strategic half of a cyber-attack mission. On the tactical side, there needs to be a determination on how to deliver the desired effect against the target and in most cases that requires the establishment of some level of access to the enemy system. Access in the cyber domain is the placing of an attack effect in such a place that it can adequately execute its mission against the target. In some cases, the target may have an address on the open internet in which case access may simply be any other internet-connected device. In others, access may be having privileged access to a device in the same organization as the target. Access can also be more stringent; some attack tools may require almost no latency between the device where it is executed and the target and require an access adjacent to the target on the same network segment. There is also the possibility that the attack effect needs to be placed on the actual system it will affect, in such cases operations to gain access to an attack position take the mission right to the intended target.

These situations requiring local target access also bring in additional risk to an attack mission. Battlefield preparation by gaining access to attack positions can happen far ahead of the intended attack date, and in those cases, the access operation requires extreme care as if discovered gaining access to the system it may tip the hand of the attacker to their intention and level of compromise within the enemy network. This is true of any access; however, the specificity of being on that actual intended target may allow the enemy to attribute not only an actor but potentially identity and motivation. Imagine attack operations that targeted Indian counterintelligence units who focused on Pakistani organizations. If an access operation were caught before the attack delivered, it is at least highly likely that the perpetrator was from Pakistan and the intention was potentially more than intelligence gathering.

The enemy target may be telecommunication control servers located in an enemy government building. Ensuring the ability to engage that target with cyber-attack effects however may require access in a much more tangential way than seen in conventional

© Jacob G. Oakley 2019
J. G. Oakley, *Waging Cyber War*, https://doi.org/10.1007/978-1-4842-4950-5_8

warfare. If we were going to destroy those systems with a missile, for instance, the only access required to launch that attack is to get the launcher within the flight range of the intended target and hit fire. In the cyber domain access to an attack position can be much more complicated. This is especially true of systems that are not internet facing, and even more complex, or even impossible, when considering systems that are closed off from another network connectivity. Gaining access to a system which can deliver our intended cyber-attack against the target could involve exploit operations across many seemingly unrelated networks in an effort to get closer to accessing the target network.

Access Tools

Access tools are those which, once installed on a cyber domain system, enable access to that system sufficient to conduct the intended attack effect against the enemy target. They are code, commands, or scripts which are tools by which those carrying out the cyber-attack can leverage the necessary attack position. Commonly referred to as backdoors or trojans, malware, and rootkits, these access tools enable delivery and execution of cyber-attack effects during cyber missions. Cyber access tools are as diverse as physical counterparts such as having a copied legitimate key to access a building without authorization a tunnel dug under a prison perimeter to break out a convict. In all cases access tools require varied levels and types of access to successfully deploy the follow-on attack effect.

Levels of Access

Access level is determined by the context the access tool has with regard to the amount of systems it applies to and the privilege it holds on those systems.

Local Unprivileged

Local access means that the access tool only needs access to a specific system. This may be due to the fact that the attack is either going to affect the local system itself or that it needs to be executed on that system but targets another. Unprivileged local access means that the tool need only provide access to the machine it is installed on and that it requires no special system level or super user context to deploy the attack effect.

Local Privileged

The only difference with this level of access is that the access tool requires privilege on the local machine to successfully execute the attack effect. Unprivileged local access is probably more common in situations where the attack tool is executed on that local machine but targets another. Unprivileged users on systems perform actions and run software all the time, and so long as there is no specific need to escalate privilege, the access tool can use that same normal user context. In cases where the attack effect will target the local system the access tool is installed on, it would likely require privileged access. With privileged local access to a system an attack tool can essentially do whatever is needed. Privileged access can allow for security software to be turned off, system configurations changed, and so on.

Non-local Unprivileged

As access to more than singular machines is required, it becomes non-local in nature but does not always require privileges to be effective. An access tool that facilitates non-local unprivileged access may not seem like it is appropriate for deploying attack effects at enemy targets; however, if those attacks involve actions like sending malformed traffic in hopes of impacting the non-local targets, then there is a possibility no privilege would be required on the non-local systems.

Non-local Privileged

Systems being attacked across a Windows domain might require non-local and privileged access such as the domain administrator account would provide, allowing the attack effect to have unfettered access to all systems within the domain. Where local access is singular to a system, non-local access continues to escalate in levels of access as the non-locality expands. That is, access with a domain administrator privilege allows an attack to impact that domain, but if the domain was one of many in an enterprise and there were administrator accounts with wider authority across multiple domains, that would be an escalation of access levels from the singular domain administrator access.

Types of Access

There are many types of access involved in cyber operations. Some cyber activities require the development of no specific access, while others require interactive access deep into target networks.

None

There are certainly plenty of opportunities for attacks between states where no access to enemy systems is required to deliver an attack effect via the cyber domain. As the world continues its push toward the internet of things and greater internetworking between states, organizations, and individuals, attacks requiring no access will increase in prevalence.

Non-interactive

Non-interactive access is a type of access to remote systems where there exists an ability for the access tool to perform actions on the host system it is installed on but not for a remote operator to do the same. This type of access is used to execute an action on the remote host, such as an attack tool being told to begin its mission, but not leverage the remote system itself. Non-interactive access tools may rely on event-driven triggers to dictate automated behavior, whereas others may wait for a command from a remote source, and others still may ask for commands at set intervals.

Event-driven non-interactive cyber access tools may wait for a certain system event to happen before executing their follow-on cyber-attack or could even be tripped due to the geolocation of the system changing a specified amount. A good non-cyber example of this type of scenario would be a sea mine. Once deployed the sea mine just sits there until a ship (hopefully an enemy one) bumps into it, depressing its trigger mechanism and initiating the attack on the ship.

Access tools that wait for commands might simply sniff local network traffic for certain types of traffic, and upon seeing that traffic, read it and operate on the commands contained within. There has even been malware that constantly checks a specific Twitter account set up for it where operators are able to send command and control to it via social media. Here the access tool is waiting for a certain Twitter message from the attacking organization to then launch its follow-on attack. This scenario is closer to that of a remote-controlled explosive device, placed and armed but not detonated until receiving a command from the troop with the controller.

Lastly, those access tools ask for commands, reaching out to a listening post at certain intervals to see if there is any new tasking such as to uninstall or execute attack effects. This type of access tool is often referred to as a beacon and is widely used in security operations and for malicious intent alike as it can be easily disguised and difficult to detect.

Interactive

Access tools that are interactive allow for more varied interaction with the system they are on. Where the non-interactive tool allowed or interaction with itself, interactive access tools allow a remote operator to perform actions specific to the machine it is installed on. These types of access tools allow the remote operator to do things like leverage system commands or run software installed on the system in essentially the same way a user sitting at that device's keyboard would. These types of access tools are more likely to require a privileged level of access to afford the remote operator as much access to the system environment as possible. This is not always necessary for attack effects; however, if detailed information must be surveilled from the system or more dynamic interactions are required for the execution of an attack effect, interactive access tools may be necessary.

Imagine a cyber-attack was to be launched on a system, but only once the identification of that system's user was confirmed and that the window for execution was extremely small. An interactive tool would allow a remote attacker to do things like take a picture with the web camera, view the documents opened by the user, and see what web sites, like social media, that user was using. All of these attributes would allow the remote attacker to immediately determine if the accessed machine belonged to the intended user and was thus the desired target. Using other access tools which wait or ask for commands may still allow for the picture to be taken and commands to be queried with result in the names of documents or sites visited, but if they happen across several ask or wait periods, they may not be agile enough to identify the target and deploy the attack effect in the desired time window.

Access and Target Relationship

There are categorical facets to the required level of access and the resulting attack operations they pre-position for. In some cases, no access into enemy cyberspace is required to facilitate the attack effect. Many times, access is likely needed in some fashion, and that access must not be discovered or the attack effect will ultimately fail. Less likely are accesses which, even when discovered, still enable successful attacks. There must be a predetermined point during access operations where a certain level of detection or attribution requires that the attack be aborted or ceased.

No Access Required

The non-cyber example of an attack that does not require any access other than a point to launch from are intercontinental ballistic missiles (ICBMs). ICBM launchers are kept within the boundaries of the attacking state and can essentially strike anywhere in the world upon execution of an attack. Though there have been developed countermeasures capable of intercepting some ICBMs, they are still an attack effect in the physical domain which requires no additional access to deliver adequate effects against chosen targets.

The cyber example of an attack effect which requires no additional access for appropriate launch points are denial-of-service (DoS) attacks against internet-facing assets of the enemy state. DoS attacks disrupt communications and computing capabilities typically by sending immense amounts of traffic (sometimes malformed) to devices in order to alter or deny their ability to function as intended. These are common on the internet as they are relatively unsophisticated in nature and can be directed from an internet point of presence into a state's cyberspace against that of an enemy state. Though this would require access to the internet, there is no need for an access operation to exploit to an attack position in preparation of the attack as the internet can be connected to from nearly anywhere. This does not mean that all DoS attacks occur across the open internet or even always between states, but they do represent the type of cyber domain warfighting attack activity that would need no proceeding access operations facilitated by exploitation within the cyber domain.

Access Noticed, Attack Prevented

The worst thing that can happen to an attacking state in cyber warfare is for their battlefield preparation to be noticed by the intended enemy victim or other entities. Being noticed during battlefield preparation in cyberspace and other domains can result in the attack effect being prevented due to enemy responses or called off due to political or safety concerns.

As a non-cyber example, I think the Bay of Pigs represents a highly illustrative scenario for how attempts at access were noticed and the attack was prevented. In this case many phases of the attack were too far along to be aborted and the attackers were disastrously defeated. In planning and aiding a rebel assault in the Cuban Bay of Pigs, the US CIA had done much work to prepare local rebel forces to engage in an attack against the Soviet-backed Cuban government and military. The plans had been discovered, including the locations from which the attacking rebels would land and attack, and instead of catching the Cuban government and military by surprise, the rebels were killed or captured and the entire operation was a huge embarrassment for the CIA and the US government. There were many errors that led to the totality with which the operation failed, including assumptions that the US President at the time, Robert Kennedy, would allow the United States to be drawn into the conflict once it started and back the rebels, which also did not happen. The crux of the mission failure though was that the intention and method were discovered ahead of time which allowed the enemy to lay a trap for the aggressors instead of being the victim.

For an access operation to be noticed is actually much more likely than in the case of a highly planned covert operation by the CIA. It at least does not rely on counterintelligence and spies. A simple antivirus or logging mechanism can detect exploitation attempts required to gain access in preparation of cyber-attacks, and that alone could spell failure to the entire operation. Imagine an exploitation attempt aimed at deploying an access tool in an enemy power plant was discovered on extremely sensitive devices due to the exploit causing parts of the system to crash and a security pop up alerting the operators of those devices to the issue at hand. Both manual and automated responses to this security system alert are going to not only end the ability of the cyber access operation to preempt an attack but have the possibility of incurring other impacts on cyber operations against that state as well. There is even the potential that security alerts caused by false positives or even other actors lead to reactionary responses by the defensive mechanisms of the target which could make executing the attack effect impossible.

Access Noticed, Attack Carried Out

Though an access attempt that is noticed often ends an attack operation in one way or another, there are still times where access is noticed yet the attack is still carried out. There are several reasons why this could be. Sometimes mission success and cost may still be deemed acceptable despite being noticed. There is also the potential that there is no other choice but to continue carrying out the mission due to its importance. There are other reasons as well, some specific to the domain in which the attack occurs and some agnostic of the warfighting domain.

The raid that led to the death of Osama bin Laden is a great example for this type of scenario in recent history. Access was required to conduct the raid on the compound bin Laden was hiding in. That access was enabled in this case by stealthy special forces helicopters which flew deep into Pakistani airspace in the dead of night to drop the SEAL team responsible for the raid on and in the compound. As the helicopters landed to deploy the raiding party, one of them crashed due to unforeseen consequences of hovering over the high-walled courtyard and resulting quick loss of altitude. Local residents around the compound noticed the helicopter crash, as too did the individuals within the compound. Despite this, and an ability to abort the raid then and get the SEALs out, the mission continued. Obviously, this mission was extremely important, and the result of the raid ended up being a great success. Despite being detected during the access portion of this attack operation, it was carried out and the intended target received intended effects of being neutralized and identified.

Examples within the cyber domain will never live up to the heroics perpetrated during the bin Laden raid, but there are certainly instances where access activity on enemy systems might be noticed but not completely compromise mission success. Imagine the same scenario as before, where the alert caused a reaction by the enemy which thwarted the attack. This time though, the access tool was deployed with persistence in the actual firmware of the system, below the operating system. As such, the enemy state wipes the device and thinks it has rid itself of the threat but upon being turned back on the system reinstalled the access tool configured with a cautiously long call home delay. As long as the intended target and attack effect were suitable to the delay required by this type of stealthy persistence than the mission could still be considered a success since an attack effect can still be executed against the intended target. This example is a little different in the iteration of the detection and attack process than the physical example of a special forces raid. Where the attack was noticed and that same activity simply continued in the raid, the cyber-attack was able to survive detection in another way by going quiet and returning to access and attack activity when safe. The timelines in these missions is what drove the reaction to being noticed, but in both cases, the attack effect was successfully executed due to the resilience of the access and the mission itself.

Access Unnoticed, Attack Aborted

Being noticed by the enemy is not the only reason some access operations or their subsequent attack effects were called off. Sometimes it is observation by the attacking party that leads to something being noticed which leads to the operation being aborted. It is a very valuable asset to operations in all domains of warfighting to know when it is appropriate to cease access or attack actions despite the effort remaining unknown to the enemy or target.

Operation Eagle Claw was a rescue mission to be carried out by special forces on helicopters. The helicopters had to be moved undetected within their fuel range of the target so that the raid could be successful once executed. The helicopters successfully made it to the access point from which the mission would launch known as Desert One. However, unforeseen environmental issues led to breakdowns and operational issues with the helicopters. Though eight were sent and the mission had been planned to go ahead as long as at least five were available on that day, the mission was cancelled even though six helicopters still operational. The decision was made that despite earlier assessment that six helicopters would be enough for the mission to be a success, the rate of failure in the helicopters at the staging area led the mission commanders to decide there was too great a risk of breakdowns that would happen mid-mission and called it off. The enemy never noticed the helicopters or special forces staged within flight range of the target, but the conducting forces determined from what they themselves had noticed that the mission would potentially fail, and lives would be lost so it was aborted despite successfully going unnoticed to the access point.

In cyber operations, environmental and situational conditions noticed by those carrying out the mission can also lead to it being called off despite stealthy access being accomplished. One reason of many may be the time window. If the operation successfully gained access to a launch point for the cyber-attack but the process took too long and target fidelity had been lost or confidence in the attack effect otherwise lost, the execution of the attack could be called off. Additionally, with the deep penetration of multiple networks needed for some cyber operations, there are always concerns with reliability. Despite having access tools deployed and talking deep into enemy networks across multiple organizations to get to a target, if they are too finnicky or connections too unreliable, the mission may be aborted. The most appropriate access position available is no good if the timing of the attack is thrown off by unknown deltas due to the access unreliability. Timing plays a huge part in strategic decisions to conduct attacks in the cyber domain and others, and as such any attack effect whose ability to fall within mission specified time Windows might responsibly be aborted.

Access Unnoticed, Attack Carried Out

Lastly, we have those operations whose access efforts go unnoticed and their attack effects are executed against the target as intended. Sometimes access operations rely on other efforts to keep from going noticed, and this is equally the case in all warfighting activities. History is full of deception and distractions which enabled access to be gained and attack effects launched from that gained position.

The D-Day landings at the beaches of Normandy are probably the largest unknown example of this in warfighting. Ignoring the fact that the forces were certainly noticed once they landed on the beach, the landing fleet making it across the English Channel and beginning to land troops and equipment without being destroyed at sea certainly constitute adequate access for the mission without it being noticed ahead of time. Further, efforts by the allies actually led to enemy forces being redirected away from the intended point of attack, saving countless lives and likely leading to the success of that mission. In fact, there was an entire effort known as Fortitude South where the allies made it seem they were going to land at a completely different part of the French coast. A fake army with fake equipment made of wood and balloons was stood up across the English Channel from this farcical landing spot, and the feared General Patton was even made commander of the landing force to lead credence to the charade. It was successful, and the mission on D-Day was not discovered ahead of time and turned the entire war.

A successful cyber engagement involves similarly gaining access without detection prior to launching an attack effect and maintaining that access until the attack is intended to happen. There are countless examples of compromises, some likely state committed and others by non-nation actors where the compromise of a network and resulting access was never identified until after the attack effect of that operation was launched. Probably though, the best of them are those where the attack effects and the access that led to it were never attributed to the cyber domain of warfighting to begin with. Such success in cyber warfare would mean attack effects could be delivered without far-reaching consequences or implications beyond the cyber domain and represent the tip of the spear in cyber war. After all, if the enemy doesn't even realize its networks were used to enact some attack on them, they won't be looking to address security within their networks and already established accessed within the cyber domain can facilitate further warfighting or intelligence collection operations if necessary.

Attack Surface

The totality of enemy assets that have a potential to enable appropriate access for cyber-attack effects to execute against the intended target makes up that organization's attack surface. Typically, this attack surface consists of other systems in the cyber domain, which upon exploitation can get the attacker closer and closer to the target. This is not all that makes up the attack surface however, as the physical domains of warfighting often facilitate enabling efforts for cyber operations. This could be in the form of physical access aided exploitation operations where a human introduces exploitation or access tools to an enemy network where cyber domain-based exploitation had been unsuccessful. It can also be the case when range of communication protocols such as Wi-Fi or Bluetooth require closer physical access than internetworked attacks.

A good analogy for attack surface is road systems. Imagine the only way to get to the enemy target was via the road systems of the enemy state and all you had was the address of the target and a rough location. Your vehicle has a missile launcher capable of striking this enemy target from a thousand feet away, so you have to get relatively close as well. Without a map or GPS or overhead imagery of the enemy road ways, it might take quite a while to reach the target. The road you initially enter the enemy state on probably doesn't take you straight to the target so you will have to make many changes to other highways and take different roads to finally get close enough to launch the missile at the target. You may even go down several roads and take highways which end up being dead ends and don't get you any closer to the target.

Exploitation across networks is very much like this. You may have several network accesses into the enemy attack surface; however, you may spend hours, days, or longer going from network to network across the enemy attack surface looking for suitable access to the target. Just as the roadway scenario had dead ends, it is possible you exploit into systems and networks that end up not furthering the cyber operation toward target access and an attack point at all. Also, just as no one road took the vehicle to the target, it is likely that a cyber domain exploit operation will have to go from seemingly unrelated network to unrelated network in attempts to get to a position capable of seeing the target address. The enemy system may not connect to the internet. Maybe the target system is a power plant control device with no ability to connect out to the internet. Being a power plant control device though it lives on a network with other devices, some of which analyze power meter readings passed to them by systems in an adjacent network. Those power meter data aggregation devices also don't talk to the internet but they do talk to power meters across the military installation they are installed on, and some of those meters may be attached to the barracks on the installation where troops do have laptops with internet access and use the building ethernet to play games against each other which also uses the same switching device as the power meter for the building.

In this scenario an attacker could essentially exploit and install backdoors across each of these segments ultimately giving access, from an internet-based pivot point into the barracks, on to the power meter network, exploit the aggregation machine, and ultimately provide access to the non-internet accessible power plant control system. This example is fairly rudimentary, but it illustrates that just because a target within the cyber domain does not have an ability to access the internet itself, it can be accessed. In many cases that machine likely talks on a network with some other machine that talks to another network and on and on until finally something can reach the internet or is otherwise accessible to the attacker.

Scoping Access Operations

This does make cyber access operations and their required exploitation somewhat unpalatable to most warfighting doctrine. The attack surface required to engage the target may consist of devices, systems, and users so disparate from the military cyber system that Title 10 battlefield preparations against them seem unethical and perhaps without authority. Worse yet access operations may often lead to dead ends, meaning that the Title 10 battlefield preparation sections were all for naught against certain portions of the attack surface. The perception of cyber-attack operations can be a bit troubling when cyber exploits were conducted against schools, non-combatants, and church's or non-profit charities in attempts to find networks that may lead to the intended target, but which yielded no results.

What if the target shared a backbone network connection with a hospital and the hospital was easily exploitable but the target network not so? In warfare medical targets are off limits according to international convention, and battlefield preparation falls within Title 10 of the US Code pertaining to warfighting actions and authorities. Does this mean that the hospital networks are off limits? I don't think this rabbit hole has been fully considered or explored by warfighters regarding cyber domain warfighting activity and it probably needs to be. It may seem innocuous and not worth the Geneva Convention scrutiny that an attack leverages access gained in a hospital network to move into a neighboring network containing the target to pre-position attack tools. After all, it isn't like the attack itself was launched against the hospital.

On the other hand, what if one of the exploits used against a hospital system to further access toward the target network crashed the machine as exploits are apt to do? What if that system controlled life support to several individuals and they ended up dying? Now this scenario looks a lot more like a violation of the Geneva Convention and an international war crime. Now it seems like the hospital network perhaps should have been considered out of scope for Title 10 operations despite the convenience. I would point back to the hunt for Osama bin Laden; in many occasions, his location was known with some decant fidelity to be within certain cities or locations; however, the United States and its allies didn't go dropping nuclear bombs on those cities in hopes of killing Osama bin Laden. This may seem extreme, but it highlights the simple point that just because an attack could be enabled from a certain position in the enemy attack surface doesn't mean that position should be within the scope of Title 10 operational authorities.

ROE for Access Operations

Just as attack effects require strict rules of engagement to ensure that the attack activity falls within the strategic intent as well as ethical and legal bounds of acceptability, so too do access operations. It is important that the end justify the means and that no unnecessary exploitation operations occur if at all possible in the placing of access as attack positions. Similar to the ROE we discussed in the previous chapter, before the onset of access operations, there needs to be established determinations for success and failure of access operations so that they may be monitored and halted as necessary. As we covered earlier in this chapter, preparation of the battlefield within the cyber domain must follow international convention and the authorities that cover the law of war. Access operation ROEs should outline how to approach the enemy attack surface in furtherance of an attack on a Title 10 target so that it is just and appropriate. Using non-combatant pivot or attack positions to place and execute an attack effect against enemy forces is potentially a war crime just as it would be to bomb a hospital and a school to open up lines of fire for machine gun nests.

Summary

In this chapter we covered the concept of access as a facilitator for attack effects against chosen targets. We outlined the different levels of access and types of access required for different types of attack scenarios. Additionally, the risks associated with detection of access operations and the resulting impact on the ability to conduct cyber-attacks was explored. Lastly, the concept of attack surface was detailed, as was the need for appropriate scoping and ROEs regarding exploitation operations against such attack surface.

CHAPTER 9

Self-Attribution

Earlier we covered enemy attribution and the process of attribution by which indicators of compromise eventually lead to identification of an actor and its potential motivation so that appropriate responses can be directed at strategic targets. Conversely, self-attribution is something that is typically avoided, especially when it is unintentional. Self-attribution happens when any portion of the attribution process yields an indication of perpetrated cyber activity. When a victim attempts to complete attribution of actors conducting cyber warfighting activity within its networks, the focus is on fully attributing that enemy such that responses can be responsible and appropriate. Where self-attribution is concerned, each phase of the attribution process can have huge impacts on the ability of the perpetrating party to continue to carry out warfighting activity in the cyber domain.

It is also important to recall that in the case of Title 10 warfighting actions specifically, there is the expectation of eventual acknowledgment and culpability. This is true for most Title 10–type actions; however, there was also the concept of covert action with its own special rules. In covert action the perpetrating organization is never going to acknowledge its role, even in the face of seemingly factual evidence. Similarly, intelligence gathering activities have no mention on whether or not acknowledgment of the activity is ever expected or required. Even in the case of Title 10 attack actions, acknowledgment of such activity has far-reaching ripple effects with impact on seemingly unrelated efforts. As such, intentional acknowledgment which attributes cyber-attack efforts must be carefully considered and planned. Further, in most cases, unintentional attribution of any fidelity is something to be avoided.

There is a careful analysis that should go in to when self-attribution should occur, just as the impacts and issues with unintentional self-attribution must be known, and appropriate responses to unintentional self-attribution prepared. The first consideration that must be had is whether or not self-attribution is ever acceptable. If the answer is never, then every precaution must be made to avoid it and implications and response actions must be planned accordingly in case self-attribution does occur. If the answer is yes, self-attribution at some point becomes acceptable the determination of when and

© Jacob G. Oakley 2019
J. G. Oakley, *Waging Cyber War*, https://doi.org/10.1007/978-1-4842-4950-5_9

how is most responsible and beneficial must be made prior to intentional self-attribution. The decision to self-attribute cyber domain activity must weigh operational concerns, political ramifications, strategic impacts, and moral dilemmas.

Unintentional Self-Attribution

We will first take a look at those cyber domain activities which at no point support intentional self-attribution. Intelligence gathering, battlefield preparation, and covert actions do not reach a point during or post operation where self-attribution by the perpetrating state is beneficial. That isn't to say that at a certain point, if self-attribution does occur, it does not have an extremely negative effect on the operation. As an example, imagine intelligence collection activity was happening on enemy cyber systems over 10 years ago and several of the tools did not uninstall correctly when the mission was over. If the perpetrating state was attributed this long after operations had already ceased, it would not affect the operation itself nor likely prove costly at all to the perpetrator. At worst it probably would lead to some awkward political issues had the two states mended relationships.

In the case of battlefield preparation, so long as attribution does not happen until that prepared battlefield has been used by an attack effect, the impact of self-attribution would be low. It is when self-attribution of battlefield preparation activities hinders the performance of the follow-on attack effect that self-attribution is dangerous. With regard to covert action however, there is essentially never a point where self-attribution of such activity is without heavy consequence. The nature of covert actions and their inherent need to avoid being tied to the perpetrating state lead to a continuous effort at avoiding any attribution.

Examples of Self-Attribution

We will walk through some examples of self-attribution for both intelligence gathering and battlefield preparation cyber activities. Attribution at each phase of the attribution process has varying impacts on these cyber activities, and we will explore how self-attribution occurs at that point and the issues it leads to for the related cyber operations. Covert action will not be covered in these examples as it is simply avoided at all costs and the impact of attribution at any phase of the attribution process is unacceptable. I will also not cover the motivation phase of the attribution process, where the motivation of the perpetrator's actions is understood. This is because when the end effect of the cyber activity is not a cyber-attack effect, which has already happened, attribution of motivation is tantamount to guesswork and does not support doctrinal responses.

Indicators of Compromise

This phase of the attribution process relates to the discovery of a clue or clues to potential unauthorized behavior which is not yet tied to another, or at least not tied to enough others to indicate the presence of an actor.

Intelligence Gathering Activity

In the cold war and probably other conflicts, practitioners of espionage utilized dead drops and markers to pass along information without ever meeting. For example, maybe there was a bench at a particular park that, when it had a chalk mark on the side, meant information was waiting in a predetermined spot to be picked up. This is a way intelligence was moved from one individual to another in hopes of avoiding detection. This activity might be considered to have disclosed an indicator of compromise if the mark was not whipped off by the party that picked up the intelligence and it was later noticed by someone unrelated to the intelligence gathering and passing activity. By itself, this mark on the bench does not represent the threat of an actual actor in the country gathering and passing intelligence, but it is certainly an indicator of compromise that can eventually lead to that picture of compromise being painted and attribution completed.

Cyber domain intelligence-gathering activities have the same necessities as physical activity in that the intelligence has to make it back to those who act upon it. This means getting intelligence collected on cyber systems out of the network it was found on and back to systems controlled by the perpetrating party for processing and analysis. Taking data out of networks like this is known as exfiltration, and if it is not conducted carefully, there is a chance that the network traffic related to the exfiltration of data and intelligence might stand out against the normal network activity. The network administrators of the enemy network might see some of his exfiltration traffic, and it may simply appear that there is a slightly heavier than normal flow from several machines in the network to web sites on the internet. Since this could be due to user activity or malicious activity, it does not on the face of it belay a cyber compromise, but it is a potential indicator.

The biggest repercussion to self-attributing even a single indicator of compromise is that it has the potential to tip off the victim to the activity. Even if a search for the compromise doesn't begin off a single self-attributed indicator, it does frame future observations by the enemy which may lead to quicker attribution later. For example, the chalk mark on the bench by itself doesn't raise much alarm; however, if the same type of mark started appearing with regular intervals or appeared in almost the same manner on benches outside several government buildings, it becomes much more concerning. There were no additional types of indicators that led to this deduction, simply the continued observance of the same type of indicator. The danger to operations when even a single indicator being discovered in the cyber domain is similar. Perhaps the exfiltration traffic was not very concerning at first as it was close to the same amount as normal users and seemed to go to a normal web site. If the victim was to search for that same type of traffic across a wide span of time or across multiple hosts and discovered, it happened at regular intervals or only across certain machine types not there is an elevated threat the victim will perceive and potentially act on. In this scenario too, there was no second type of indicator, only further observation of the initial indicator based on the fact that it was noticed in the first place.

The only real mitigation that can be offered for avoiding self-attribution at the indicator of compromise phase is to not be noticed. As we have just shown, even a seemingly uninteresting indicator by itself can lead to wider attribution of cyber intelligence gathering operations. There are two main ways in which cyber operations tradecraft aids avoiding detection. First, the perpetrator can simply be more careful and stealthier and put a focus on non-attribution nearly as high as accomplishing the mission. The decision to embrace this type of tradecraft may avoid detection but also may lead to more mission failures due to time-constrained issues. There is also the concept of acting within the noise, which when done correctly can be a more efficient way of avoiding self-attribution. If artifacts and clues of the perpetrating actor are indistinguishable from normal behavior, they don't indicate anything to the victim.

In the example where the bench was marked to indicate intelligence was placed at a predetermined location for pickup, the actors could have behaved differently and potentially avoided creating indicators of compromise. After all, writing on the sides of benches at a park may be discreet, but it is certainly not normal behavior for park-goers. If instead the individual who was dropping off the intelligence fed ducks bread and left the bag of bread on the ground under bench and walked away with a certain amount of slices in the bag, the person picking up the intelligence could simply pick up the bag and throw it out as if a concerned citizen and then go pick up the intelligence. Taking it a step further, the dropping individual could even use the number of slices left in the bag to communicate to the picking up party. Maybe two slices meant "do not get the intelligence, we are being watched", one slice meant the intelligence was placed, and three slices meant break contact permanently.

In the cyber intelligence gathering activity, the slightly abnormal web site visitation traffic cued the organization as an indicator. What if instead of that, the exfiltrating party simply used compromised machines to message a Facebook or LinkedIn account and offload data and intelligence that way. Now to the administrators, they just see a user doing excessive browsing on social media sites (which the actual user of the box also probably does). Even if the administrators took corrective measures and contacted the user of the machine to tell them to calm down their social media behavior at work, it is unlikely to make anyone suspicious and thus discourage further prosecution.

Battlefield Preparation

In medieval battlefields, as well as in other times and places, the use of markers to indicate range measurements has been used to help dial in fire by archers and siege engines such as catapults. To prepare the battlefield scouts might stack stones at observable positions in known intervals to help the friendly forces range in their attacks. This type of activity certainly falls within the definition of battlefield preparation and as such is a Title 10–type activity and not a Title 50 one as it does not afford for any collection of intelligence, it has the sole purpose of benefiting attack activities once they begin. Here the indicator which may lead to self-attribution is the stack of stones. If the enemy forces did not know there was an encampment of soldiers across the battlefield, but their scouts found the stacked stones, it might lead them to further investigation. Finding a single stack of stones may indicate the presence of humans in the area but not indicate that the scout is actually on a battlefield prepared by another force for attack. Similar to the intelligence gathering example, if the other stacks of stones were seen by the scout in patrolling the area, it would potentially lead to the deduction that there was something else going on. No new indicators were present, but finding the one stack and then identifying it to be the same as others in other locations at seemingly regular intervals might allow the enemy to believe there was something malicious going on.

There are actions an attacker within the cyber domain can also do to prepare the battlefield for eventual attack activities. Altering firewall rules slightly so that an attack effect, when executed on a system being used as an attack position, is more effective would fall within this category. A firewall change that was innocuous enough by itself may seem more malicious if it was determined to also happen across other systems, all of which afford access to sensitive areas of the organization. Here the single rule change which didn't point to much of anything by itself may be interpreted as preparation for something more nefarious of the same change was discovered across the network.

Discovering indicators of compromise related to battlefield preparations has the damaging potential to take away the element of surprise. Even though sole indicators may not highlight the actions of an individual actor, they may be enough to tip off enemy forces that some form of battlefield preparation has been conducted, even if it is not clear that the preparation was specific to them as the enemy. In the medieval range stones example, the enemy may not think there is an enemy force around or that they are in fact on part of a prepared battlefield, but the stacked stones do indicate at least a man-made item. If the force was attempting to avoid detection itself, it may take greater care to avoid detection or even change course and route. Any of these things impact the ability of any follow-on attack to be less successful and just because an indicator was discovered, not even having pointed to a malicious actor.

The changed firewalls might also be identified as simply a widespread error within the network and be fixed by the systems administrator as they are viewed as unnecessary. Again, the simple discovery of the indicator can lead to behavior by the target which hampers an attack ability. The enemy administrators may think there is nothing malicious or even an actor related to the firewall rule change, but they still acted upon the discovered indicator of compromise. This self-attribution is completely unspecific to the attacking party, and yet it affects the ability for warfighting activity in the cyber domain just as it can in the physical.

The stacked stones used for range finding stood out because once again they were abnormal to the surrounding area. If the forces had instead picked natural land marks or perhaps made less obviously man-made markers for range finding, the enemy scouts may have not discovered them and the battlefield would remain prepared, the element of surprise maintained, and the enemy actions unaltered. In the cyber domain example, if instead of adding a new firewall rule to the list of rules the preparation was to expand an existing firewall rule to include allowing for traffic related to the attack, it may have gone unnoticed. Once again staying within the noise is a great way for the activity, cyber or otherwise, to remain undetected by intended victims and not impact the ability for attack effects to be deployed.

Actor Association

Actor association is when multiple indicators of compromise are associated together as representing the same actor. As opposed to just an indicator of compromise, self-attribution of this level means the enemy knows that there is an actual unauthorized presence conducting activity.

Intelligence Gathering

Carrying on the initial example of the chalk marks on benches used to indicate and help pass intelligence between individuals, further indicators of compromise can be associated together to indicate the presence of unauthorized actors and activities. The chalk mark itself was innocuous if not odd and maybe did not set alarm bells ringing immediately. But what if on the ground behind the bench with the chalk mark was a divot in the ground as if a cone-shaped stake had been there. Also, in the trash can down the path from the bench, a cone-shaped stake with a cavity big enough for a roll of film was discovered. Any three of these indicators by themselves are not likely to be associated to an actor attempting to move intelligence, but together they represent continued self-attribution.

If we look to exemplify the same scenario in the cyber domain, the initial indicator of odd exfil traffic must be correlated to other individually benign indicators. In addition to the traffic, let's say those same machines started to experience a slowdown in performance, as if they were working harder than they should be. Also, let's say that abnormal remote user credentials were found on the same and other machines in the network. Alone, slowdown in performance could be attributed to anything, with malicious activity probably not even near the top of potential responsible candidates. Abnormal user keys could be explained away by people using other people's machines in the company or even administrative activity. Together with the abnormal firewall rules though these indicators associate together to represent a definite unauthorized actor within the network. This level of self-attribution by the perpetrating actor can be much more costly than any of the indicators by themselves.

The impact of self-attribution at this level can be much more detrimental to the end goal of intelligence gathering activities. When it is only an indicator that is attributed, reactions by the target may as a byproduct affect the operational end goal. In the case of self-attribution establishing that there is an actor present, the reaction by the victim is going to be a specific attempt to thwart that discovered actor. The association of indicators to an actor means a doctrinal change in the ability for the victim organization to respond. When only indicators are self-attributed, the victim organization may use information about those indicators to improve actor agnostic security measures for the organization. On the other hand, when the presence of an actor is established by association of indicators, the victim organization can improve actor-specific defensive measures which are likely to end the actor ability to exfil or move intelligence.

Mitigation of individual indicators of compromise revolved around avoiding detection via improved tradecraft. Being quieter or living within the noise were good ways for indicators to not be noticed. When attempting to mitigate the risk to operations posed by indicators being associated to one actor, the perpetrator must do everything possible to appear unrelated to that identified actor. This means changing tactics, techniques, and procedures as well as resources leveraged to collect intelligence. If multiple indicators have been discovered and associated as a specific actor, the perpetrating party must avoid further association with that established actor profile.

In the case of physical passing of information, this might mean changing from marking benches to marking tables or from using hollowed out stakes to some other form of information storage. They key is change, and to change techniques and tactics as often as possible, so that even in the face of indicators being associated to one actor, the perpetrating actor prevents its actions and their resulting artifacts from pointing back to the same entity. In the case of the cyber example, the change needed to mitigate actor association can happen any number of ways. Perhaps instead of having abnormal credentials used to gather intelligence on the same machines used to send that intelligence out of the network, the actor has a more disjointed approach where intelligence is gathered and aggregated on one group of machines and then passed internally to separate machines responsible for getting that data out of the network. The intelligence gathering actor might also change the methods of exfiltration every so often to appear different and avoid being associated as one singular actor.

Battlefield Preparation

Piled stones placed as range markers may seem unthreatening, but what if other indicators were discovered that seemed related to the same activity of battlefield preparation and thus a singular actor. Perhaps the scouts this time see the stacks of stones and then also observe trenches in the distance and some trip wires and traps across well-worn paths troops are likely to use. Now the scouts are likely to report that it appears a hostile force of some kind has been preparing the area to hinder troop movements and sway the battle.

In our cyber example of battlefield preparation, maybe the administrators, in addition to noticing the odd firewall rules, also find further artifacts that when paired together are easily associated together. If the administrator also found that several important security system logs were set to delete every few minutes and that some unknown executable files had been found on some of the machines with odd firewall rules as well, it would certainly seem like evidence of a singular actor preparing the machine for something, or at least efforts to hide certain activity.

The impact of self-attribution resulting in actor association for intelligence gathering activity may be the end of a stream of important information. When it happens with battlefield preparation activity, it can endanger the success of attack effect missions as well as the livelihood of those carrying out the attack. Upon seeing the range stones and trenches and tripe wires, the scout now reports that there is a specific hostile force somewhere preparing to do battle. In this case the enemy forces may avoid the prepared battlefield altogether, meaning if the perpetrator still wanted to do battle, it would be in a less advantageous environment. Worse yet, the enemy scouts may perform counter-attack activities unbeknownst to the preparing forces. If the enemy scouts decided to say "move the range stones to make attacks less effective," they may change the placement of trip wires and traps to instead affect the preparing party as well. They might also find a way to use the trenches dug in battlefield preparation to their own advantage, turning the work of the preparing party against them. In the case of the cyber example, the discovered binaries on systems may be copied and forensically analyzed. Best case result of that might be the enemy knowing how and what was targeted by the follow-on attack activities related to the cyber domain battlefield preparation. Worst-case scenario, those executable binaries reveal publicly unknown attacks and tools which the enemy now can turn against the preparing forces or other targets.

Mitigation of association for battlefield preparation activities within the cyber domain can benefit from routine changes to methods and tools used in an effort to avoid being associated with a singular actor profile. Additionally, such activity benefits from being carried out as close to the attack effect as possible so that there is little time available for the battlefield preparations to be discovered and impact the ability of the preparing forces to conduct their cyber-attacks. Where intelligence gathering activities may go on for years, cyber-attack effects are likely short in duration and likely or even intended to be discovered. As such, a more efficient way of avoiding association may be limiting the time preparation activities, and associated artifacts are exposed to potential detection instead of putting high amounts of work into disassociation of those activities and indicators.

Actor Identification

The identification of the actor is a determination using indicators of compromise and related information to not only associate activities with an actor but to identify who the actual individual or organization is behind those activities.

Intelligence Gathering

In our espionage intelligence gathering scenario, actor identification can be relatively straightforward. The individual dropping off the intelligence may be a local source and not indicative of who is collecting and processing the information; if the person who picks up the intelligence is identified, it might reveal what organization is behind the effort. At a minimum witnessing who picks up the information identifies the singular agent behind the activity. Less obviously, if the intelligence were discovered and collected by the victim after it is dropped in the hidden stake but before the person who picks it up gets there, identification of the perpetrating party may be possible based on how specific the intelligence contained in the take is. If the target of intelligence gathering is specific enough, it can indicate who the customer of the intelligence is likely to be.

In the cyber example of exfiltrated intelligence, it can be more difficult to determine the identity of the actor gathering the intelligence simply based on where the data goes. If the person who is picking up the espionage at the park is identified, it can be easily verified what the person's identity is. In the cyber example, even if the external systems where the data is being sent are identified as belonging to a given organization or state, that information does not necessarily indicate who the end customer is. As we covered when discussing attribution in general, in cyber it is very easy to obfuscate and alter, and while the destination addresses of the intelligence gathering exfiltration might belong to China one minute, it could change to belonging to Ireland the next if it is in a cloud-hosted environment. Therefore, identification of an actor in the cyber domain more heavily relies on self-attribution through the type of information being gathered and taken out of the network. Even unspecific intelligence can give a range of potential identities for the collecting actor, and the more specific the intelligence, the easier to tie to certain potential actor identities.

When self-attribution in intelligence gathering activities leads to the actual identification of the perpetrating part, there are certainly political and perceptual ramifications that may result. There are also operational problems that arise when an enemy is able to identify who is trying to collect information from them. The worst thing that can happen to intelligence gathering activities in the cyber domain and the physical domain is discovery and identification by the enemy without the perpetrator's knowledge. If this happens, then the enemy victim organization can perform misinformation and counterintelligence efforts with extreme efficiency. Passing misinformation and incorrect intelligence can undermine the state security at every level of the perpetrating nation. Troops can be sent to the wrong locations, strategic warfighting decisions are made based on enemy provided facts, and false or inaccurate senses of security can be established by the intended victim.

The best way to avoid self-attribution resulting in identification of the perpetrating party is to first and foremost avoid leaving behind indicators of compromise or performing activity in ways which ease association to a singular actor. When that doesn't work and the enemy has determined that an actor is present, it may be appropriate to completely cease operations and/or attempt to remove artifacts and indicators. This tactic only works if the perpetrator knows the enemy has decided there is an actor present, in the physical domains, intelligence gathering activities certainly attempt to adhere to stealth to avoid being identified. In the cyber realm, identification without admission is extremely difficult to do with any reliable level of fidelity. Still, cyber intelligence gathering activities should do everything possible to avoid self-attribution resulting in even cursory attempts at identification by the enemy.

Battlefield Preparation

Self-attribution identifying those conducting intelligence gathering activities means the perpetrator is either denied further intelligence gathering activity or worse yet is potentially mislead via counterintelligence activities of the enemy. When battlefield preparation reaches the identification phase of the attribution process, self-attribution may result in the perpetrating state failing to secure strategic goals or even become the target of hostile actions itself.

Now, upon realizing that there is a potentially hostile actor around the prepared battlefield, the enemy scouts conduct further reconnaissance. In doing so they observe siege weapon technology specific to only a few possible adversaries and even see several shield and banner emblems actually indicative of the specific state those troops belong to. The scout is now able to return to its forces with an identification of the enemy who prepared the battlefield. In the cyber example for battlefield preparation, upon forensically reversing the executable binaries found on several machines, the enemy was able to determine their intent. The effect of the cyber tools discovered on enemy machines was to turn off sections of security perimeters between the victim state and the perpetrating one. At this point the perpetrating actor has self-attributed itself as being the neighboring state who was preparing for invasion through the security perimeter.

Repercussions form this level of self-attribution for battlefield preparations may have grave consequences. Upon identifying who was preparing the battlefield with trenches range markers and traps, the enemy forces could simply choose to not engage the perpetrator on that battlefield but begin marching toward another exposed portion of the perpetrating forces' territory. Not only does this rob the preparing forces of the planned strategic defeat of their enemy, it has not allowed the enemy to take over the element of surprise and march in forces on an unsuspecting portion of the perpetrator's territory while its forces wait to do battle on the prepared battlefield against an enemy force which will now never show up.

In the cyber example, self-attribution of this fidelity is likely to implicate other warfighting activities. If the enemy now knew that its perimeter was going to be unsecure and that was the location the neighboring enemy forces would invade from, maybe they prepare bombing runs and evacuations from that area. The self-attributed and unwitting perpetrator of battlefield preparations now has its forces crossing at a known location where the invasion attempt will be disastrous. Even on a less severe scale, identification of who is behind battlefield preparation activity allows for preemptive strikes and targeting by the enemy against the perpetrating state.

To lessen the issues that come from self-attribution of who is conducting battlefield preparation, obfuscation and generalization are likely methods. Limiting the exposure of battlefield preparations to discovery prior to attack is still best practice, but that is not always feasible. In such cases, battlefield preparation should be conducted in a way that identification of the perpetrating forces potentially misleads the enemy into thinking it has a different enemy than the preparing force, or that the preparation is so general that it could enable an attack from anyone and thus leaves the enemy forces to discern which among any of its potential enemies has prepared the cyber or physical domain for battle.

Intended Self-Attribution

In the case of Title 10–type warfighting activity, there is the possibility that self-attribution is an intended action. Remember that cyber-attack effects are executed under Title 10–like authorities by uniformed members of the military or their agents and under the command and oversight of the nation's military apparatus. As such, there is an expectation that at some point the state's role in the attack effect will be disclosed. This is important to stay within the concepts of just war and abide by international convention, but it is also part of the projection of power. There are two ways a state may seek to self-attribute its attack activities within the cyber domain. The activity may either be made so obvious as to indisputably implicate the perpetrating party or the nation who conducted the attack may come out and announce its participation.

In either case, purposeful self-attribution must be done when the acknowledgment of activity does not impact the effectiveness of that action or of other related actions yet to come. If announcing responsibility for a cyber-attack effect would implicate other warfighting actions yet to be executed, that announcement must be delayed until all related actions had taken place. For example, if a state announced it was able to shut off power to a city so its forces could safely move through it, and such information would belay the path an invasion force was taking deeper into enemy territory, such an announcement would need to be delayed until after the invasion to avoid impacting ongoing operations. If that same cyber-attack which crippled power in that city was going to be used across the enemy territory at different times during a conflict, self-attributing the capability to do so on purpose may allow the enemy to become more resilient to the attack effect or thwart it altogether in the other locations.

Projecting Force

Other weapons available to the warfighter allow the state using them to project force. Projecting force allows for conflict and violence to at times be avoided due to other states understanding the capabilities and not wanting to face them. Understanding how weapons such as stealth bombers and tactical nuclear weapons on submarines act as a deterrence is easy to see. Enemies know that if they conduct open aggression thata response is going to come, and it may be one which it cannot stop or eliminate. Projecting force through the cyber domain is a bit more difficult.

A bomb dropped from an undetected stealth plane is likely to be as effective on its target the hundredth time as it was the first time, and therefore displaying, using, or acknowledging the capability doesn't necessarily impede its effectiveness as a deterrent to future aggressions. Once a cyber-attack is used and then responsibly and openly admitted as part of warfare by the perpetrating state, there may be an intimidation factor associated with that action. The capability though is then likely lost for future use. Once used, and even if not announced, a cyber-attack effect is likely to be noticed. Announcing the use of the cyber-attack effect makes it certain to be noticed. An enemy state may potentially attribute a loss of power to power lines or power plants being physical destroyed or tampered with.

When the cyber-attack is announced, the enemy knows to immediately begin forensic actions against the victim systems to understand what just happened to their cyber systems and to prevent it in the future. Worse, if security products were installed on those systems, international security software vendors may now have their hands on the attack effect tools as well. Security vendors often share signatures, and announcing a cyber-attack effect such as what may have turned power off in a city means that the attack tool and potentially the access tool that enabled it are now known to the entire world and automatically caught. If there was not enough disparity between the attack tool used and announced and other prepositioned attack effect tools in other locations, this type of signature might catch them as well and ruin worldwide operations by the perpetrating state.

Clearly self-attribution has far-reaching implications, but specific to the projection of power, it can be self-destructive. Current and future enemies may now respect that the perpetrating state is capable of creating and delivering such attacks and that is in itself projection of force. However, that same effect is likely to never realistically be used again due to the dynamic nature of the cyber domain. The real strategic decision that must be made then is, does acknowledging the use of cyber-attack effects and the potential projection of power that comes along with it outweigh the other impacts such self-attribution may bring about?

Summary

In this chapter we covered the concept of self-attribution. In doing so we analyzed the already understood attribution process from the perspective of the perpetrating state. Unintentional self-attribution of varying degrees and of varying activities, including intelligence gathering, battlefield preparation, and covert action, was discussed. The consequences of such self-attribution at different levels was also covered. Lastly the concept of purposeful self-attribution and how it is part of cyberwarfare and can be used to project and impact power was detailed.

CHAPTER 10

Association

In an age of interconnectivity and within a domain of cyber centered around the internet, it should be no surprise that cyber domain activities are nearly incapable of cross or interacting with devices belonging to neither the aggressor nor victim state in any cyber warfighting activity. In most imaginable cases, the internet or World Wide Web plays a key role in the conduct of cyber domain actions. The term internet itself belies the origin of its creation for internetworking, and the Web in World Wide Web is a simple and powerful indicator to the messiness in cyber communication paths. The internet revolves around a lack of regulation and singular ownership, where devices owned by organizations and individuals all across the world communicate in common protocols.

Due to this interwoven and unregulated communication forum, it is almost impossible for a cyber domain activity to make it from perpetrator to victim without being processed or interacted with, and therefore potentially associated with, by some device external to the victim-perpetrator relationship. It is worth discussing how this fact should impact cyber operations. Is association avoidable? Should it be avoided? Is it useful to manipulate association? These questions and others relate to this issue which is unique to the cyber warfighting domain. One way of understanding this unavoidable aspect of the cyber domain is to consider an analogy using sovereign airspace. If the United States, for instance, wants to drop ordinance on another country in a declared conflict, there is certainly the potential that the aircraft which drops that ordinance did so after crossing external sovereign airspace belonging to another state or states. In such cases, it is not typical to view the various countries whose airspace the US aircraft crossed to be complicit in the dropping of the ordinance on the enemy country. In fact, in most cases the United States has alliances and other international agreements where it is allowed to fly its aircraft through other countries' airspace and is therefore not in violation of their sovereign airspace. Flying an aircraft through a nation's airspace is easily understood as not associating that country with the activity being conducted by the perpetrator.

© Jacob G. Oakley 2019
J. G. Oakley, *Waging Cyber War*, https://doi.org/10.1007/978-1-4842-4950-5_10

Unfortunately, this logic fails when applied to the cyberspace scenario. To relate the two, consider the following. Instead of flying through another country's airspace in a US aircraft to drop ordinance, imagine the US plane had to land in each country along the way. More than that, it had to land, be placed on board a larger plane belonging to the state whose airspace it needed to cross, then flown in that larger plane across the country's airspace. Next, at the border, the US aircraft would have to be moved into another of these larger aircraft, this time belonging to the bordering country, to then be hauled across its airspace. This process would be continued until the aircraft got to the border of the intended victim for the ordinance drop where the US craft would embark once again on its own into the sovereign airspace of the enemy victim and ultimately drop its ordinance. In this example association between the perpetrator and the countries whose airspace needed traversing is much stronger; after all, they actually loaded the US plane and the bomb it carried onto their own aircraft and then transported it toward the intended victim. In such a situation would it be harder to argue the associated transporting states were not in some way complicit with the attack?

Though seemingly ridiculous, the airplane scenario is very analogous to how cyber warfighting activities traverse the internet. Data which ends up exploiting, maintaining access to, attacking, or returning intelligence data from enemy systems is potentially sent from a perpetrator-controlled device, across a network of uninvolved third party–controlled devices until ultimately passing into the enemy system to perform its intended function. Each device along the way unwraps the data packet, processes the routing data used to let the packet navigate the internet to its intended destination, repackages the data packet, and sends it to the next devices along the way.

There is a tool built into Microsoft systems called tracert which will ask for a response from each device between a sending device and the destination device for the purpose of troubleshooting connectivity issues. As I write this book, I am in the United States, and if I were to use the tracert tool against an address in another country aside from one directly connected to the United States, it is almost certain that at least one device along the way that takes up and reroutes the data packet will not belong to the United States or the ultimate destination of the tracert command. This is because when you send traffic over the internet, be it tracert traffic leveraging the ICMP or web email leveraging the IP, the device you send it from does not actually know the entire path to the destination location. Typically, the device you send from only knows the location of the device which knows more paths, or routes, than it does. Consider the following abstract example of a tracert result which started from 1.1.1.1 (let's assume the United States owns this address) and ended at 5.5.5.5 (let's assume France owns this address).

1. 1.1.1.101 – This is the address of the device 1.1.1.1 knows to send traffic to for further routing

2. 1.1.2.101 – This is the address of a bigger internet service provider (ISP) bigger routing device that knows about more addresses

3. 1.1.3.101 – This is the address of a main U.S. device that knows how to rout to the U.K across the Trans-Atlantic cable

4. 2.2.3.101 – This is the address of a main U.K device that knows how to rout to the U.S. across the Trans-Atlantic cable

5. 2.2.2.101 – This is the address of the device in the U.K. that knows how to get to other countries in Europe

6. 5.5.2.101 – This is the address of a device in France that knows how to get to other countries in Europe

7. 5.5.1.101 – This is the address of a device in France that knows how to get to the specific destination address of 5.5.5.5

This routing example is very similar to how the postal mail service works. If you live in a small town and you are sending a letter internationally, your small local post office does not send the letter directly to your destination, it routes it to bigger and bigger post offices until your letter reaches one which handles international mail. From there it is sent to the foreign country where it is passed back down the chain to smaller and smaller post offices in the destination country until it ends up at the local destination of your address.

If we were sending some malicious mail to the foreign country instead, and one of the stations it passed through was a third-party country, external to our conflict, we potentially risk associating that third-party country with our actions involving the delivery of an attack effect on our target. Mail services often ban certain types of packages including weapons or explosives. In this case does the third-party country get a pass since it has a disclaimer that you are not allowed to mail weapons using its service or is there some expectation that the third party inspect the parcels for illicit contents? In a traditional mail system and the internet, association and blame center on this question of responsibility. Figure 10-1 illustrates a comparison between the tracert example and the mail analogy.

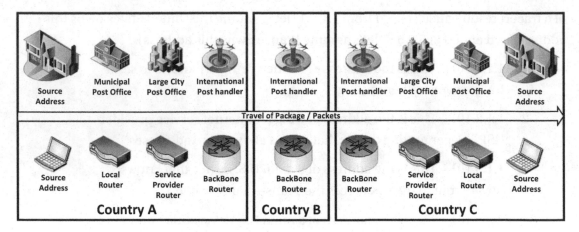

Figure 10-1. *Package/Packet Traversal Comparison*

At some point, or at what point, is a third-party country's mail service, or in the case of the cyber domain, internet routing device, responsible for the contents it couriers. Understanding the ways in which association can be implied, applied, and understood is necessary in an age of cyber warfare. Without such an understanding, the second- and third-order effects of such association cannot be mitigated or controlled. Association can result in breaches of international convention, committing war crimes and breaking or invoking alliances by implicating the potentially uninvolved.

Types of Association

The implications of association can certainly be concerning and more than worth the time to scrutinize. In fact, with the power to in the very least optically implicate a third party in warfighting actions, there are both purposeful and incidental associations which may occur during a cyber domain activity. Approaching purposeful association with measure and tact while avoiding unintentional association wherever possible is a must in cyber warfare.

Incidental

The potential for incidental association is almost impossible to avoid in many cases. Often the way in which cyber activity is conducted requires traversal through the cyberspace of multiple third-party nations on its way to the target destination. This leaves the door open for possible association of those third parties with the attack action even though it originated in a separate place. This type of incidental association is external to the target organization and for obvious reasons raises some concern for potential repercussions against those uninvolved in the conflict whose devices were leveraged in the delivery of cyber actions.

There is also the concept of incidental internal association. In this case, it is not an external third-party nation state associated with a cyber action but an internal device and/or user. In incidental internal association, it is not the devices handling and routing traffic which end up associated with the activity. Being internal to the organization, the administrators or security and monitoring staff of the organization or even nation state likely control and can forensically inspect the devices after the fact at the internet service provider level or internal to the actual target if necessary. This level of access means that though those internal to the nation devices were routing the attack activity, association can be ruled out as benign from the perspective of the owning party within the target state.

On the other hand, consider a host compromised via a spear phishing attempt in which a user opens a malicious email, visits a malicious link, and through their actions executes malicious code from an enemy state. If the attacker is careful enough, even cursory forensic activities on the compromised computer may not reveal the presence of an outside attacker. In this case the organization or state may assume the individual is an insider threat and act against them accordingly. This has many but different impacts than incidental external association but is itself worthy of careful consideration. Incidentally associating an internal device and its owner with something such as cyber-attack actions could result in that person being deemed an insider threat, traitor, or enemy plant. Those conducting cyber-attack activities must consider the ramifications of accidentally letting incidental internal association happen as it could ultimately lead to the death of the internally associated individual or individuals.

This is the best place in the book to also address a non-association-related issue that can also result in the potential firing, incarceration, or even death of innocent bystanders. In the other warfighting domains, air, land, and sea, the sovereign area belonging to a nation state is clearly defined and also likely protected in some way by a military entity. The cyber domain of warfighting consists of an attack surface for each nation made up not only of military assets and individuals but also government civilian assets and individuals. I can certainly think of a few countries where a contractor or government employee administering important devices which ended up being used to launch or were the target of a successful cyber-attack effect might be severely punished by incarceration or death if it there was even a perception the attack could have been prevented. Even were this not the case, I think in many if not all nations such an individual who did not protect or detect such an attack would find themselves jobless. International convention and laws of war may never address this issue, in any case a nation state conducting warfare in all domains, including cyber, should take care to avoid implication, associating or damning bystanders in the carrying out of warfighting actions. This is especially the case in cyber where the danger of such unintended consequences on innocents is a dynamic and difficult challenge.

Purposeful

The fact that incidental association will happen is easily understood though clearly the implications are a web of unfortunate and unintended consequences. Purposeful association is the process by which the nation state perpetrating cyber warfighting activity willingly associates that activity internally and/or externally, in one way or another, to satisfy various motivations.

For Obfuscation

Purposeful external association to provide obfuscation involves any effort to tie cyber activity, its origination, and potentially its motivation to devices, individuals, and organizations or nation states in an effort to hamper forensic efforts by the target at identifying the source of the cyber-attack. If done correctly, this type of activity can help prevent the attribution of the perpetrating state while not implicating the involvement of third parties through association. This is the difference in purposeful and incidental association—in purposeful association, the information the enemy has access to regarding where an attack came from is at least in part supplied in intentionally conflicting and complicated ways.

External to the target, this would involve an effort to utilize multiple redirection points immediately prior to launching the attack or exploitation activity as well as creating a chain of devices which redirect the traffic prior. Redirection points are simply devices placed or exploited for the sole purpose of altering the path and direction of network traffic between the perpetrator and victim. In this way, through the involvement of many dispersed and chained points of redirection, a perpetrating actor can both obfuscate its own location and actions and avoid a third party being identified as associated and potentially complicit to the attack activity. It is one thing if the attacked organization sees the cyber-attacks being launched via traffic all originating within a single third-party nation state, which may negatively associate that state with the action. On the other hand, if the redirection points are in several nation states or, even better, are coming from known cloud hosting service addresses in several locations, it is both obvious that the perpetrator is trying to cover its tracks, which protects the third parties associated with the redirection points, as well as making it unobvious where the attack actually came from.

Carrying on the postal service analogy, imagine instead of mailing attack effects from source to destination address, which potentially associates third-party states between perpetrator and target, we instead mailed our bombs to five different countries and had them repackaged and resent as if from those five countries all at the enemy state. The target will have two likely take-aways. First, it is unlikely five separate nations are mailing it the same kind of bomb attacks. Second, it is unlikely any of the five countries were the perpetrators as that would be too obvious.

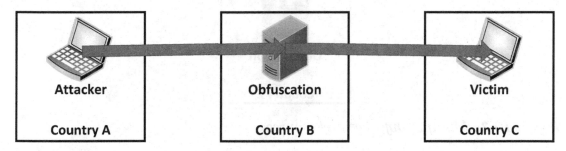

Figure 10-2. *Singular Obfuscation Resource*

Figure 10-2 represents a situation where a singular obfuscation point is used and may associate the activity irresponsibly. Figure 10-3 shows using multiple obfuscation points which presents a situation where the victim both understands that the attacks are being obfuscated and also that they are likely not from any of the obfuscation points themselves.

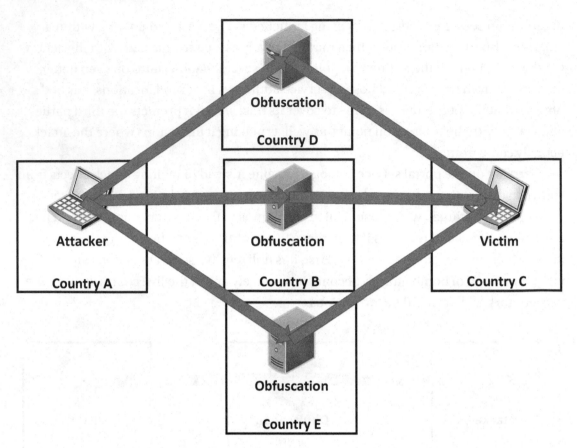

Figure 10-3. *Multiple Obfuscation Resources*

Purposeful internal association in an effort to obfuscate is more about protecting access to the target and an ability to carry out the intended warfighting activity than to prevent self-attribution, as that is more relevant in external obfuscation. Internal obfuscation involves creating redirection within the target state organization or network to attempt associating attack effects with one set of compromised hosts and current and future access operations with others. In this way the perpetrating state hopes that upon launch of a cyber-attack effect, that action will be forensically tied to hosts that have nothing to do with the way the network was initially accessed. In this same manner, the perpetrator's presence in the network can be obfuscated to simply complicate forensic activities by the target state as well. In both cases such internal obfuscation via association helps to avoid self-attribution as well as enabling resilience in the ability to access the target and deliver attack tools prior to the attack being launched.

To Distract

Whether done internally or externally, using association to distract the target of a cyber activity is in the gray if not on the bad side of ethical implications, especially in regard to attack effects. Where obfuscation aimed to prolong identification of the perpetrator through varied associations, distraction aims to clearly associate a singular third party in hopes that the effort spent by the target in researching, engaging, or responding to that third party will benefit the perpetrating state. As with obfuscation, the purposeful nature of association to distract afford the perpetrator more control over the association aspect of cyber operations and the resulting impacts.

Distraction through external association can be responsibly done. Irresponsible distraction would be one that resulted in the association of a third party with the cyber activity to the point of even implicating they are not only associated with, but the likely origin of that action. In this case the third party is at risk of facing warfighting responses from the target state due to the poor tradecraft of the perpetrator. Responsible distraction would be one which made the same clear association with a third party but where that third party is not likely to suffer warfighting repercussions. Aside from the method of association is the chosen entity to associate with the activity.

For instance, if the United States attacked Pakistan with a cyber-attack effect but made it appear that the attack was associated with India, such purposeful association would be irresponsible. Pakistan would likely not waste much time looking into the validity of that association and may even simply use the fact that the attack appeared to originate in India as an excuse to launch its own warfighting actions. In a different scenario, if the United States attacked Sweden but made the cyber-attacks seemingly associate with Norway, it would be much more responsible.

Sweden, knowing Norway has no reason to seek aggression against it, would certainly take a long time to dig into the details of the cyber-attack and its association with Norway. In such an example, Norway and Sweden are even likely to cooperate to determine who the real perpetrator was. In this case, if they ever even determined it was the United States that launched the attack, the obvious association with Norway would have distracted the target long enough for the United States to accomplish further actions, in the cyber realm or others, knowing its target was off its trail for some time.

Accomplishing distraction through association internal to a state is accomplished in the same way as before and has the same responsible and irresponsible potential executions. If the attacker made strong associations with the attack effect coming from a random user in the target organization, it could be irresponsible as that individual may be responded to as an insider threat or traitor. If instead the association was tied to some other organization within the enemy state, the association would serve more as a distraction while the enemy dug into why it appeared one of its organizations was attacking another. Imagine a scenario where devices owned by the US Navy were clearly associated with carrying out cyber-attack effects against the US Army. There would be no warfighting response by the Army against the Navy, but the association would distract the Army by forcing them to investigate why this appeared to be the case. In such examples, the forensic efforts needed to rule out the association in fact tie up multiple organizations including the target and the associated entities in the enemy state as they determine why that might be.

To Self-Attribute

We have already covered the concept of purposeful self-attribution, but it is worth tying back into the association concept. Purposeful self-attribution can come through near immediate declaration by the perpetrating state of what cyber warfighting activities were carried out. This is not always ideal as perhaps the warfighting activity is not desired to be announced yet as it might implicate or endanger other operations simultaneously going on or planned in the future. Purposeful association offers a way to skirt some of the negative repercussions to outright declaration of cyber warfighting activities, especially political ones. It can do this while still avoiding unintentional associations and the second- and third-order effects that might result. If a state strongly associates its warfighting activity within the cyber domain as coming from itself, but does not openly declare the actions, it allows for the enemy to, with a high level of certainty, know who carried out actions against it. This avoids inappropriate responses to potentially associated third parties. It also allows the perpetrator to openly refute any claims of the attack by the target on the international stage to dance around any political issues while still projecting force to the enemy.

As a Weapon

With all the potential ramifications of association, both purposeful and incidental, it is pretty clear that there is a potential for the perpetrator to leverage the association of cyber-attack effects with certain entities as a weapon in and of itself. In this case, the goal of the perpetrator is to illicit responses by the target against the associated entity in furtherance of the perpetrator's strategic goals.

Using external associations in this manner is a tweak on the concept "The enemy of my enemy is my friend." In this case though, I want to encourage my enemies to become enemies of each other. Imagine a country wanted to launch cyber-attack effects against Russia, but also wanted to illicit cyber warfighting responses against another enemy it had in China. Now, China and Russia are openly pretty friendly; however, both have a strong reputation for meddling in the cyber domain of other countries. Getting Russia to think a cyber-attack came from China with enough fidelity to incur an actual warfighting response against China by Russia will take more than the efforts discussed so far in obfuscating and distracting mostly through choice of redirection. In this case the perpetrating state of the attack against Russia will want to make it look like it didn't just come from China but that it was China. This could be done by establishing an association with China through strong attribution of the actions leading up to the cyber-attack as being tied to a known Chinese actor. The perpetrator would research a specific Chinese actor, its historical activities, tradecraft, and tactics and try to understand its motivation and use similar tools as well. In this way, the perpetrating state so strongly associates the cyber-attack effect with a specific Chinese actor that Russia has no choice but to respond against China. In this way association was weaponized to not only attack one enemy but get that enemy to lash out against another enemy of the perpetrating state.

Where weaponizing association external to the target involves getting one state to act against another, weaponizing internal association would be intended to have the enemy state attack itself. This may be a potent weapon if there was an enemy commander who posed a significant danger to the warfighting efforts of the perpetrating state, or an enemy scientist posed a similar danger to war efforts. Association can be weaponized to make the enemy state act against its own resources.

Imagine the development of the first nuclear weapon was ongoing in today's world, with Oppenheimer still directing the Manhattan project in an effort to create a nuclear bomb. Now imagine that an enemy of the United States was able to launch cyber-attacks that hampered this effort. Moreover, that enemy was able to so strongly associate those attacks as having been launched by Oppenheimer himself that the United States considered him a threat to future development and an agent of a foreign enemy. This association means that not only was a cyber-attack launched against the nuclear bomb development program, but that successful or not, association was weaponized to convince the United States to depose their own most valuable resource in the development of a nuclear bomb, the lead scientist and director of the program in

Oppenheimer. The association and subsequent actions against Oppenheimer would probably set the US nuclear program back further than even a successful cyber-attack effect.

Summary

In this chapter we covered the concept of association and how it is an unavoidable aspect of operations within the cyber domain. Through example scenarios involving cyber and non-cyber domains, the concept of association and routing of cyber traffic was illustrated. Incidental association and its impacts were covered as were different methods for purposeful association and the benefits and drawbacks to warfare, international convention, alliances, and state and individual livelihood.

CHAPTER 11

Resource Resilience

There are many diverse resources that coalesce into a warfighting effort within the cyber domain. For strategic and tactical decisions to be made regarding cyber activity and its impact on larger warfare or even individual missions, those resources need to be readily available and at the disposal of commanders and combatants alike. The resilience of these resources in the face of many challenges and obstacles is critical to cyber warfare. The sheer amount of resources that could be leveraged in war even within the cyber domain is limited only by the imagination; however, we will stick to common and easily understood resources which are generally categorized into being either operational resources, support resources, or personnel-based resources.

As the coming sections will highlight, the cyber domain of warfighting presents an extremely dynamic and volatile environment for the resources required to operate within or from it. Understanding how the loss of each of these resources impacts the ability for cyber-attack effects to be delivered is essential to successful cyber warfare. Without the knowledge of what these resources are, how they may be lost, the impacts of their loss, and potential mitigations, a state cannot confidently engage in cyber war. Lacking this understanding, the warfighter cannot operate or be supported, the decision makers cannot rely on capabilities or intelligence, and the state risks losing its ability to project power from or within the cyber domain.

Operational Resources

These resources are those which are technologies leveraged within the cyberspace of the target state to carry out exploitation, access, intelligence gathering, and attack activities against enemy cyber systems.

© Jacob G. Oakley 2019
J. G. Oakley, *Waging Cyber War*, https://doi.org/10.1007/978-1-4842-4950-5_11

Exploits

First, we need to ensure that exploits are not confused with vulnerabilities. Vulnerabilities, though leveraged in attempts to gain access to cyber systems, are not resources as they are not created, managed, or maintained. A vulnerability is simply a flaw in the target system. An exploit is the ability to take that flaw and turn it into an effect on the target system that benefits the entity executing the exploit. Unfortunately for the resiliency of exploit resources, they are at the mercy of both challenges to the operability of the exploit as well as the existence of the vulnerability itself. If either is affected, the result might be an inability to exploit the system. Think of a facial recognition that can't tell the difference between some faces and pictures of those faces. This vulnerability is exploited by people who print out pictures of legitimate personnel to get unauthorized access through the facial recognition system. This exploitation could be disrupted by either the company that makes the technology realizing the flaw and updating software to fix it or the organization seeing someone using the printed picture of employees and stopping the exploitation process itself.

In the cyber domain, a likely scenario for the loss of an exploit as a resource is that the security industry itself discovers the vulnerability that the exploit leverages and does something to fix it. Depending on how the fix occurs, it may be possible that the exploit can be tweaked to still achieve the same results, or it may be that the exploit resource is no longer available. The vulnerability can also be discovered by other hackers besides the perpetrating state leveraging the same vulnerability to attack systems. Whether the other hackers are state sponsored, amateurs, or organized crime related makes no difference, if they get caught, the security industry will analyze how they exploited their target systems. In the very least, this will result in the vulnerability being addressed and may even completely rule out any potential for a workaround tweak to the perpetrating state's exploit resource if it was similar at all to the one in the discovered hacking operation.

In these likely examples, the perpetrating state was not caught carrying out its operation so there were no second- or third-order effects related to the loss of the exploit as a resource. A more impactful situation would occur should the perpetrating state use the exploit in hopes of placing a cyber-attack effect on an enemy system and get caught doing so. In this case, not only does the perpetrating state lose the exploit as a resource but potentially tips their hand to the intent of the mission it was used in. Even worse, there is a chance the exploit and related methodology can be used to tie the operation where the exploit was caught to other operations by the perpetrating state. Imagine the same exploit was used to deliver cyber-attack effects to several enemy organizations. If on the last organization, the exploit was caught, it could be used to discover and attribute exploit activities against the other organizations and the planted cyber-attack tools would also be discovered and lost.

To mitigate the loss of individual's exploits as a resource to the warfighter involves a careful balance between operational requirements and risk. Each time an exploit is used, it potentially is the last time it will be available as a resource. This chance is extremely elevated when the exploit is used to deliver cyber-attack effects as they typically announce the presence of cyber activity and invite investigation. There is also a trend in cyber operations in general to save effective or custom exploitation tools until they are really needed. In an offensive security assessment, this might be for big ticket items that improve the assessment; in warfare it might be saving a particular exploit for a high-value target. In not using the exploit resource, the risk that the underlying vulnerability is discovered gradually increases over time. At the end of the day, weaponizing a vulnerability into an exploit is done for a reason, and each commander and decision maker should carefully weigh the impacts of both using that resource and holding on to it in regard to completing missions and maintaining the resource for when it is needed.

Access Tools

Once a system has been exploited, in many cases the perpetrating state will want to return to that system or to remotely interact with it in some way. This requires that some code be kept running on that system as an access tool that the state can leverage. In the case of a cyber-attack effect, this could be due to the tool being put in place far ahead of the actual attack and needing to be communicated with to execute the attack effect. In intelligence gathering the system may be a source of regular updated information the state wishes to continually have access to. Similar to how an exploit as a resource was impacted by both its own viability and also the existence of the vulnerability, access tools are reliant on several aspects which all pose different resiliency challenges. An access tool has code it relies on to execute what commands are sent to it, it has to have some form of communication so that it can deliver access, and in many cases, it has some form of persistence on the target system to survive power cycling. Issues with any of these access tool aspects can impact its availability as a resource.

A likely way the use of an access tool as a resource is impacted is the access tool code is no longer executing on the target system. If the tool was not persisted and was simply running in the volatile memory of the system, it would be gone upon that system rebooting. A system might reboot intentionally by users or administrators or unintentionally due to something like an update or power outage. In either case if the access tool had no method of persistence, it would be gone from the system and no longer a resource the warfighter could leverage. The persistence method itself is also liable to change or discovery in the same way an exploitation vulnerability is. Either the security industry discovers the persistence method and begins addressing it or some other malicious code uses the same persistence and gets discovered. Worse than simply losing an access tool resource due to a machine restarting, in this case the access tool itself may be discovered and forensically dissected, potentially impacting any missions using that or similar access tools.

More impactful than the loss of execution for an access tool is the discovery of its communication methods. If a target state discovers odd communications coming in or out of its networks and ties them to access tools on machines, the result could be worse than simply losing the access tool as a resource. In this situation, the perpetrating state which installed the tool might not know that the enemy is on to their activities. If the access tool is being used to gather intelligence, the enemy might begin feeding misinformation which would be interpreted as legitimate. Discovery of communication methods can also be used to determine the location of other copies of the access tool on other target systems by the specific enemy or even globally if they ultimately pass the data to the security industry.

Mitigating the loss of access tools, both in singular instances and in widespread discovery, is necessary to maintain an ability to pull back information, deliver other tools, and execute them on enemy systems as part of cyber warfare. There are many clever ways to make access tools more resilient. Whenever possible, persisting an access tool on a system so that it gets executed after reboots should be avoided to remove one aspect of an access tool that may be discovered. The code running on the system can be made resilient to some forensics by being made to decrypt only when running in an environment that matches its intended target. In this way, moving the access tool to another device to dissect it will result in an inability to look at its code. The tool itself could also be made tamper resistant and simply delete itself when attempts to access it happen in any way not specifically prescribed. In this way, an access tool may be discovered, and the access to a machine itself lost but other enemy systems accessed in the same way are potentially safe. The best way to make access tool communications resilient is to make them blend in with typical behavior of the enemy network as much as possible such that they do not invoke interest of security personnel, and even if they do, searching for the likeness of the access tools communication would result in devices doing normal communications as well and slow down investigative efforts that would prevent the access tool from being leveraged as a resource.

Attack Tools

This last operational resource I will cover is obvious in its value and intent, deny disrupt degrade or otherwise negatively affect the target system. Depending on the strategic intent behind the attack, the tool itself can be inherently very resilient or especially not so. Some cyber-attacks can be very general in their mission. Consider an attack to delete data gathered by an enemy system. A tool to do this is likely not very complex, data on most systems can be made unavailable through corruption or deletion in many ways including native operating system commands such as "del" on Microsoft Windows or "rm" on Linux and Unix variants. Once a system has been exploited, if the attack tool can be as simple as executing existing operating system commands to achieve the required effect, that attack resource is resilient as it is unlikely to be affected since it is part of the underlying target system. Where things get tricky is when the attack is complex or surgical in nature. If instead the strategic goal was to alter the enemy collected data to misdirect the enemy, simple deletion will not do. A specific tool might have to be created that is able to interact with the data type the enemy system produces. In this case, the ability to alter the enemy data is very specific and less resilient.

A likely loss of an attack effect centers around the vulnerability of the target of that attack. Since all cyber-attack effects require some level of vulnerability exploitation to be possible, they run the same risks of exploits. More so, there is also the likely potential that the target itself will incidentally become altered in a way that makes the original attack methodology invalid. In our example of needing to develop a custom tool to alter data collected by an enemy system, if the target system simply changed the way it wrote data to use disk space more efficiently, the way the attack tool accessed the stored data may no longer exist. In this scenario the attack tool still executed fine, but it no longer affects the target data in the intended way which means the strategic value of the attack resource is reduced or lost.

A more impactful resource loss could occur if the enemy discovered a flaw in its system that was likely to be leveraged in an attack. Now instead of the attack simply failing, the enemy is ready for it, knowing it is an attack vector that may be leveraged.

In such case, the enemy puts itself in position to monitor and understand the attack methodologies of its enemies as it can lie in wait, knowing where an attack may come from and learn more far more about the attacker tactics and tools than if it simply fixed the issue due to normal patching and upgrades instead of identifying it as a cyber-attack path. This puts wider operations at risk in a cyber war.

There are times where extremely specific and tailored attack effects will be necessary in cyber wars. In such cases they should be used as infrequently and efficiently as possible to avoid being tied together or disrupting wider operations. Mitigating the loss of attack effects and improving the availability of this type of resource is most enabled by approaching attack effects from as broad perspectives as possible, using uncomplicated, native, and replaceable attack effects where possible and when they still achieve desired strategic results. Further, strategic decision-making about when to use cyber-attack effects should incorporate the complexity of that attack effect and risks to its resiliency, continued availability, as well as other ongoing operations that would be compromised if it were discovered.

Support Resources

Where operation resources are used within enemy cyberspace, support resources are those that enable warfighting operations to interact with that enemy cyberspace and the operational tools within it. Support resources are the infrastructure required to carry out cyber warfare and are analogous to supply and communication lines in traditional war. These resources are represented in the cyber domain by obfuscation resources as well as frontend and backend infrastructure. In both traditional and cyber war, the availability of support resources is a major concern. The main difference being that in traditional war, the onus is on those support resources being defended from enemy attacks, whereas in the cyber domain, the onus is on avoiding discovery or attribution.

Obfuscation

Obfuscation resources are those which exist in the cyber domain between the friendly and enemy cyber assets and are involved in the obfuscation of operational activities in an effort to avoid their detection or attribution. This is typically accomplished through redirection of the communication methods between the perpetrator and its operational resources. This redirection requires leveraging assets that are not associated with the perpetrating state to alter the communication protocols, paths, and procedures to prevent discovery of that communication, attribution of that communication to the perpetrating state, or the tying together of multiple communication paths or operational resources. An easy way to do this is to purchase internet hosted cloud services and installing virtual machines on them responsible for obfuscating the flow of communication from operational resources back to the perpetrating state. This is a practice common in offensive security assessment such as penetration testing where the assessor wants to disassociate various activities from each other they may pay to have a virtual computer hosted in several different countries and, for instance, exploit the target from one, and have the access tool communicate to a separate one to attempt dissociating the two. Cyber warfighting operations can operate in the same way using third-party redirection to obfuscate cyber domain actions.

A likely way that this obfuscation through redirection resource could be lost is when the device or devices being used to do the obfuscation are lost. If the obfuscation resources are virtual machines redirecting communications hosted in cloud providers, this could be because the traffic to the device was deemed malicious or inappropriate by the provider and they simply terminated the virtual machines. If the obfuscation resources are real or virtual computers, the loss of the obfuscation resource might simply be due to power issues or failure of whatever tool is installed on those machines to handle and/or alter the communications going through it.

A very impactful way obfuscation resources can be lost is when they are discovered by the enemy or even worse attributed back to the perpetrating state. Discovery of obfuscation resources by the enemy also potentially puts them in a place to use this new understanding of how the perpetrator operates to tie together diverse missions against itself and potentially other targets at a huge detriment to the perpetrator's ability to conduct cyber warfare. If the enemy knew where the attack is coming from, in the cyber domain or any other, it is a problematic loss of capability, and as such obfuscation resources are extremely important to the success of warfighting operations despite their being more infrastructure than weapon.

To avoid the loss of obfuscation resources as a whole and mitigate the impact of individual redirection losses, there needs to be varied and leveled obfuscation efforts within the cyber domain. It is also important to do as much as possible to ensure that loss of obfuscation and redirection infrastructure does not lead to the loss of operational resource through either discovery or lack of communication lines. Obfuscation and redirection resources should be configured in a way that they have secondary and tertiary means of continuity of communications between operational resources and the perpetrating state operators using them. These obfuscation resources should also be varied to the extent possible to ensure that discovery of one does not lead to the discovery of others both within the same mission set against a particular enemy and in global operations against many target sets.

Frontend Infrastructure

To conduct cyber warfare, the perpetrating state must at some point have a presence on cyber systems with access to the internet. This frontend infrastructure consists of the resources that handle the receipt of communications from operational resources once they are handed off through whatever obfuscation means were utilized. When access tools reach back to this frontend infrastructure, those specific resources are called listening posts. When instructions are being sent from the perpetrating state to the access tool, which is waiting, there is no need of a listening post as the tool itself is listening. In both cases the frontend resources are required to send and receive the communications, instructions, and collection from operational resources in enemy cyberspace.

Though important these resources are much more likely to be dependable and need less in the way of mitigations to guarantee resiliency. After all, they exist within the control of the perpetrating state and any failure of frontend infrastructure systems is likely due to environmental issue as much as warfighting ones. A listening post resource is likely to fail because of an error in its code requiring a reboot or a power outage in the area it physically resides, or any number of other operational considerations faced by civilians and military cyber systems alike.

More impactful but less likely is the tying of the frontend infrastructure resources to an actual cyber-attack effect conducted against an enemy. This likely would also require failure of obfuscation resources. No matter how it happens though, this type of resource failure means that the perpetrating state makes itself and its frontend infrastructure targets of its enemy's cyber warfighting efforts. This would require a minimum a complete overhaul of frontend infrastructure and obfuscation resources to allow for continued cyber operations. Such failure also means that the perpetrating state could be identified and called out on the international stage for its actions in the cyber domain at a point where it was not ready to disclose such activity.

Improving the resource resiliency of the frontend infrastructure is in part highly reliant on the successful implementation of obfuscation resources. It also requires the implementation of availability and integrity assurances. Though the frontend infrastructure itself is a resilient resource, the fact that without it all resources past it cannot be interacted with or leveraged means careful considerations must be made. Guaranteeing infrastructure availability and the subsequent availability of other resources communicating through it are integral to strategic decisions and tactical operations.

Backend Infrastructure

Frontend infrastructure may be the conduit to and from the internet and enemy cyberspace for cyber warfighting activity, but actions within the cyber domain also require a backend infrastructure as a resource to process data collected by cyber operations and about them. This data falls roughly into two categories. There is that which was intentionally collected as intelligence through cyber activity in enemy cyberspace. There is also data about operations that can be used to further improve both tactical and strategic efficiencies. The second type of data, operational data, that is processed by backend infrastructure includes items such as how targets were accessed, when, what issues were found, and problems with other resources such as communication issues through certain obfuscation resources or issues executing exploit resources. Collecting and processing this information is a resource itself to cyber warfare, as is obviously gathered intelligence. Both are generally made available to the perpetrating state in backend resources after they have traversed from operational resources on enemy systems, through obfuscation resources and the frontend infrastructure.

Like with frontend infrastructure, backend infrastructure is also within the control and protection of the perpetrating state and as such faces high resiliency. Though not very likely, an impact that could happen to backend infrastructure is that the operational data from previous operations, detailing who, what, where, when, why, and how, could get lost or corrupted which would mean that it was no longer a resource to be leveraged by the cyber warfighters. This would impact tactical efficiencies but would not likely lead to a disruption in cyber warfare activity.

Very impactful would be an issue in the backend infrastructure resource which leads to the loss or corruption of intelligence gathered or of battle damage assessments from cyber-attack effects. In this case the loss of the resource means that strategic decisions are uninformed, and the effectiveness of previous missions is unknown and cannot support future strategies. Safeguarding backend infrastructure as a resource available to the warfighters and decision makers is integral as it is the point where leaders are informed of the cyber warfighting effort. Mitigating the loss of this resource should be carried out through redundancy and planned continuous operation.

Personnel-Based Resources

Unlike the other resource categories, personnel-based resources do not revolve around maintaining a technology or device as a resource but instead are related to humanistic attributes involved in cyber warfare.

Skill

The resource of skill is the ability for human operators involved in warfighting activity within the cyber domain to adequately interact with technological resources and carry out operations. Without skilled operators to carry out cyber missions, the technological resources which make up operational and support resources are next to useless. A strategic decision maker or commander may decide to employ one operational tool or the other, but that decision is based on an expected performance out of that operational resource. The humans operating those resources must have sufficient skill to employ those resources in the expected manner and allow for the highest level of strategic and tactical success in the cyber domain.

The most likely way cyber skills as a resource can become unreliable or unavailable happens in the same way any specialized skillset fails. Over time, without regular use, skills atrophy. The greatest danger to the proficiency of cyber operators is gaps in the use of their skills in carrying out cyber operations. Any specialized skill, cyber or otherwise, takes time to develop. Unfortunately, in many military settings, individuals rotate as a part of regular existence after periods being stationed in one place or another. Someone with highly developed skills is likely to atrophy almost completely in the years a rotation of station may bring about. There are many other reasons individuals who carry out cyber operations may have their skills atrophy due to lack of use, but military duties certainly bring about challenges to the resilience of such a resource as skill.

More impactful and more difficult to mitigate than the atrophy of skills is when they become obsolete. Given the fast-paced evolutions constantly occurring with technology involved in the cyber domain, there is always a chance that the enemy targets themselves or otherwise involved technologies change. This change could be in such a way that learned skills by the perpetrators are no longer viable for conducting cyber activity on the systems. If this occurs, there is potentially a need for the operators to completely retrain before being able to effectively leverage operational cyber resources again, seriously hampering the perpetrator's warfighting capabilities.

Mitigating these impacts to the skills of human operators involves appropriate operational tempo. Cyber operators should be engagingly employed to keep up in their proficiency. This must be done in a way that doesn't overwork those resources and also affords them the time needed to carry out enough research and training to stay on top of potential technology trends. This balance allows for skills to be maintained and ensure that they evolve with changes to stay tactically proficient.

Tradecraft

Where skill is the ability for human operators to hack enemy systems, tradecraft is the resource which allows those operators to conduct missions effectively and to not get caught. Good tradecraft allows for the accomplishment of cyber warfighting missions in adequate timelines while maintaining appropriate levels of stealth and avoiding attribution. Where skill initially comes from training and is honed with real-world experience, tradecraft is harder to develop as it is more a decision-making process than a memorized and proficient task. Tradecraft does have the benefit of not degrading like skills do without use. The benefit of being experience based means that tradecraft is more permanent once learned.

A common way tradecraft can be eroded as a resource is through lapses in judgment during training and operations. Where repetition enforces the needed skill level to accomplish a task, it dulls the sharpness of tradecraft-based decisions and observations. Repeating the same task over and over can lead to complacency and overconfidence. These issues lead to a cyber operator adhering less strongly to good tradecraft and putting operations and other resources at risk.

Worse than complacency and lapses in judgment is when tradecraft is blatantly ignored. This can occur when warfighters in the cyber domain disregard good tradecraft in efforts to accomplish missions in faster timelines, please superiors, or appear more skilled and achieve career advancement. The impact to a perpetrator's warfighting capability when operators are put in a place where their tradecraft is sacrificed is the potential forfeiture of all other resources. Poor tradecraft by cyber operators can lead to access, exploit, and attack tools being discovered, obfuscation infrastructure being lost, and frontend infrastructure being attacked. It is also important to note that at times an operator may have all intentions of following good tradecraft practices but be told by decision makers that mission goals or other issues like potential loss of life are important enough to risk loss of cyber resources.

Tradecraft is best developed and maintained through engaging cyber operators in missions which do not lead to complacency. This can be done through avoiding too much repetition and varying operational duties. To avoid a disregard for tradecraft, military organizations should strictly enforce tradecraft-related infractions. These organizations should also take steps to ensure that cyber operators do not feel pressured to throw caution to the wind in efforts to speed up mission success or career progression. Further, cyber operators should be regularly made aware of the impacts bad tradecraft decisions can have on other resources involved in cyber warfare to maintain an appreciation for the importance and far-reaching impacts of their actions.

People

Lastly and more importantly than tools, infrastructure, and skills involved in cyber warfare are the warfighters themselves. As a resource, cyber warfighters are difficult to come by, finding those who will sacrifice themselves for their country, complete military training is hard enough. Out of that pool of warfighters, finding those with a knack for cyber operations who can complete in-depth technical training to become ready to carry out cyber warfare is harder still.

It is unfortunately commonplace that such talented individuals are drawn out of the military sector and into industry where their talents, leadership, and work ethic are extremely valued. This retention issue is a serious challenge for military and government organizations hoping to grow personnel pools as a resource for conducting cyber operations. There are always those who wish more than anything to remain in service of their nation's security and that keeps some willing to stay in military or government occupation. Others see the higher salaries and more varied options of industry as an opportunity to better their quality of life. Altruism aside, this is a very real problem for maintaining readiness to fight cyber wars.

More impactful than losing such professionals to industry where they still contribute to the nation and even potentially to security as contractors is when such talented individuals become disenfranchised. This can happen for any number of reasons, probably chief among them being overworked and under-recognized. Extremely talented individuals carrying out warfighting missions in the cyber domain can easily overwork themselves, duty is a potentially intoxicating excuse to keep working and lead to operators being burned out. Leadership and commanders can also be too mission focused and forget the importance of the operators themselves, pushing more mission completion without regard to the risks of losing those operators.

Like any organization, those that are responsible for carrying out cyber operations must take care of the people who do it above all else. Without those people, there is no warfighter to carry out war in the cyber domain. Recognition should be given when appropriate, personnel should not be overworked nor allowed to overwork themselves. At the risk of sounding cliché, people are the greatest resource available in cyber war and should be protected as such.

Summary

In this chapter we covered pertinent examples of the various resources needed to conduct cyber war. These resources range from those operational tools installed on enemy systems, the infrastructure that allows interaction with the enemy cyberspace, and the operators who leverage them. The resiliency of each resource was discussed, covering likely and highly impactful scenarios for the degradation of that resource as well as mitigating factors. The resources covered categorically represent what is needed to carry out cyber war at a high level and does not represent the totality of resources available.

CHAPTER 12

Control and Ownership

We have established various resource types involved in cyber warfare and their importance to the success of the warfighter and the effectiveness of commander and decision makers. We will now cover the concepts of resource control and resource ownership as well as their uniquely amplified impact in the cyber domain. The threats to resilience and mitigations to them covered in this chapter cover for the most part threats posed to cyber warfare resources by the operating environment and defensive capabilities of the enemy and industry security apparatus. Loss of resource control and ownership are exceedingly more dangerous to the mission at hand and to overall success of waging a cyber war and represent loss of capability containment and potential damage to innocent non-combatant individuals and systems. Loss of control and ownership also potentially lead to state-developed capabilities being brought to bear against itself or its allies by enemy targets.

Resource Control

Resource control is the ability to start, stop, direct, interact with, and manage a given resource and its activity. Losing control of a resource, in any domain of warfare, occurs when that resource is still being used or active but no longer being wielded by the perpetrating force. Though upon destruction, a warfighting resource is no longer at the control of the perpetrating state, it is not actively being utilized by another entity or acting on its own without control and will not be covered under resource control. Destruction of a resource is considered final, if destruction is complete, and not under the purview of resource control and the factors that mitigate the loss of resource control. The other qualifying attribute of resource control loss is that though no longer under the direction of the original wielder and owner, the resource itself is not being recreated simply re-targeted.

© Jacob G. Oakley 2019
J. G. Oakley, *Waging Cyber War*, https://doi.org/10.1007/978-1-4842-4950-5_12

Think of the Soviet warfighting equipment left behind in Afghanistan when the USSR finally decided to pull its ground forces out of that country. Thousands of AK-47 assault rifles and other weapons were now under the control of local Afghan tribes. This is a loss of control of those individual resources because they were not all destroyed and were now being used by other forces, enemies in fact of the Russians. What is worth noting in this scenario is that though the Afghans not had at their disposal thousands of AK-47s, tanks, heavy machine guns, and other weapons, they were still not in a position to now create their own. When the AK-47s became unserviceable or tanks broke down and other weapons failed, they would be discarded, and the Afghanis would then once again be without those resources as they had no way to recreate the resource themselves.

The United States suffered a similar loss of resource control when ISIS forces took many weapons left behind for Iraqi forces by the United States and used them against non-combatants, US allies, and troops. Similar to the Afghanistan example, the ISIS fighters had no capability to replicate the US weapons left behind and used them until they no longer worked, at that point discarding them. If the ISIS forces ran out of ammunition for a particular US weapon, it would be discarded; if a US Humvee broke down, it was likely discarded. In this way loss of resource control can be seen as temporary, lasting as long as the resource itself is likely to last.

Resource control is not limited to a loss of the resource where it falls into the hands of an enemy or other operator. There is also the concept of containment and a loss of control where the resource is not in the hands of a particular external operator but is no longer under the direction of the perpetrating state. This loss of control can still be enemy initiated. If you consider a drone, or unmanned aerial vehicle (UAV), there are many examples and even open source information on the internet on how to jam communications links to UAVs and drones. If the enemy is unable to take over control of the drone but is able to hamper its ability to take direction or fly resulting in its crash, control of that resource has still been lost.

Resource control can also be as benign as losing the ability to communicate with a GPS satellite. The satellite may still perform its GPS mission but without control from a ground station may be unable to adjust orbit to avoid a collision or falling into the Earth's atmosphere. Similarly, without enemy involvement but more dangerously, loss of control could also be represented by the automated tracking and firing mechanism in the Phalanx CIWS radar-guided 20 mm cannon engaging birds and other non-aggressive targets with fire. This is what happened when a Japanese-based Phalanx CIWS locked on to and shot down a US plane during an exercise. Thankfully the crew was safe, but this is clearly a dangerous example of control loss.

Resource Ownership

Resource ownership is the ability for a state to maintain the unique ability to recreate a warfighting capability. Once the enemy or another state is able to re-create the same capability, the resource is no longer owned by the perpetrating state. Resource ownership is more a concept of exclusivity vs. the operability concern of resource control. In traditional warfare resource ownership is a concern, but the timelines involved in an enemy being able to recreate a weapon or other warfighting resource is timely. Once a weapon system is understood enough to recreate it, the enemy still has to find the resources to manufacture the capability and then bring it to utilization. In the cyber domain, this timeline can be much faster, making the danger of resource ownership loss potentially an immediate concern.

Let's consider the first nuclear bombs developed by the United States, which were developed in a long, secretive, and herculean effort. Given the deadliness of this resource and the labor required to create it, the United States certainly would want as little risk as possible regarding potential loss of ownership. If another country or countries during World War II were able to recreate the resource, resulting in a loss of ownership by the United States, the bomb would no longer be a US-only resource. Even with such a high concern for maintaining exclusive ownership of the nuclear bomb capability, the United States still tested and even used this weapon. This was done without fear of endangering the exclusivity of the weapon because in use and in testing there is next to no information that an enemy could glean to further its own nuclear bomb efforts. There was no chance that in using the bomb against Japan the Japanese Empire would be able to recreate the capability.

Resource ownership in the cyber domain is a more immediate threat upon use of a particular resource, particularly tools. Whether an attack, access, or exploit capability, once a cyber resource has been used on an enemy system, there is a chance that it might be caught and forensically analyzed. Upon analysis the enemy will likely be able to leverage the same capability within a significantly short time window. This means that unlike the nuclear bomb example, a cyber-attack, once used, has the potential to almost immediately be turned against similar targets by the initial victim.

Resource ownership can also be lost when it is not recreated but becomes so understood by the adversary that they develop countermeasures effectively nullifying it. If a resource is no longer viable because the enemy has made it completely ineffective, it can no longer be considered a resource in that conflict and is therefore no longer a resource owned by the perpetrating state. During the raid on Osama bin Laden's compound Abbottabad, Pakistan , one of the stealth helicopters delivering the SEAL teams crashed, most of it was destroyed but the tail portion fell on the outside of the compound wall and was mostly intact. Pakistan allowed the Chinese to take and analyze the tail portion of the aircraft. If the Chinese were able to reverse engineer the stealth technology on the helicopter tail section and make their radar able to detect it, the United States would no longer own that stealth resource in a conflict with China.

Resource Examples

As we did in this chapter, we will examine the various resources and examples of loss of control and ownership for each as well as covering the impact of that loss and potentially mitigation.

Exploits

Exploits are used to gain remote access, escalate privilege, and in general manipulate a target system in ways its owner does not intend. The danger is relatively low for a remote targeted exploit resource that it is taken and utilized by an external entity. Even in possession of a tool that launches the exploit, without the ability to recreate it themselves, they are unlikely to be able to target it adequately against other systems to constitute controlling it themselves. On the other hand, tools that perform local privilege escalation can be executed on any target with the similar vulnerability. It is therefore a realistic possibility that a privilege escalation tool could be discovered on a victim system by the enemy and then taken and used by that enemy on other systems.

The loss of control over an exploit resource can also occur if a remotely exploiting and self-spreading virus begins exploiting systems outside of the intended target range. With the self-spreading virus going after unintended systems and if the perpetrating state cannot cease the weapon's activity, it has lost control of that resource. This can occur when things like device addresses are used as targeting logic for such cyber tools. The virus may be meant to spread to any target in the enemy within a specific set of network addresses; however, if one of the infected systems is taken to a place where it can communicate with a different network that uses similar address schemes, the tool may spread there too.

Losing ownership of an exploit resource is something that should be carefully considered prior to leveraging it. Cost-benefits must be weighed in the decision to use an exploit that is unique to the perpetrating state. Once an exploit is utilized, the enemy may notice it, and having captured network traffic or forensically gone through the victim system is now able to similarly leverage the vulnerability through their own similar weaponized exploit. At this point the perpetrating state has lost ownership. An exploit resource that is exclusive to the perpetrating state is one that is viewed as a zero-day exploit, in that no other entity has the same capability and the security industry does not know of the capability. This is an extremely valuable resource to be protected and safeguarded. If ownership is lost, it puts the perpetrating state in a potential race to defend itself from the same capability.

In fact, if an enemy was able to recreate a previously exclusive zero-day exploit, the perpetrating state might even decide to make it publicly known to the security industry in hopes of heading off the enemy's ability to utilize it. This is not a danger to all exploit resources, many systems I have come across in offensive security assessment are well known, decades old exploits with available patches and fixes. Just because an exploit is known and no longer exclusively owned by a state does not mean that potential targets have fixed their systems against it. If in a specific conflict however the enemy observes the exploit and instead of recreating it for themselves simply nullifies the ability for the perpetrator to leverage it against their systems, the perpetrating state has summarily also lost ownership of that resource.

As covered in this chapter, mitigating the risks associated with exploits is a tempered approach to their use. Even in situations where a perpetrating state uses a publicly known exploit against an enemy system, once the enemy learns of the exploit, they may update their systems making them invulnerable. In this case, exclusivity and ownership was not a concern, but the exploit still ceases to be something the perpetrating state can utilize. The concepts of ownership and control loss of ownership come with significant concerns of not only limiting the capability of the perpetrating state but potentially endangering others. Say a perpetrating state acts irresponsibly and lets a powerful exploit fall under the control or shared ownership of an enemy state who then uses it against all of its enemies. Does the perpetrating state share some responsibility for letting this exploit into the wild so to speak? What if criminals now use that exploit to target innocents? These questions may seem excessive due to being cyber domain activities, but they can still be warfighting actions that ultimately impact non-combatants and that is worth contemplating.

Access Tools

Of all the examples we will discuss regarding loss of control, access tools as a resource are overall the least impactful when this happens. One way control of an access tool might be lost is if the enemy discovers its presence on a system or systems and begins manipulating the access tool's environment on that system so that it behaves in ways the enemy wants. The enemy may not be able to reverse engineer the functionality of an access tool used to pull back information out of a network, but they might be able to determine what files on the system the access tool is monitoring for and collecting. If this is the case, the enemy can actually control what information is making it back to the perpetrating state that installed the access tools.

Control can also be lost without enemy intervention. Earlier we discussed how a satellite used for GPS may lose its ability to communicate with its ground station and operators. This didn't stop it from sending GPS signals but means that the control of that resource was lost. Similarly, an access tool, which beacons out to the internet every so often to receive tasking, may be on a system that is moved to a network that can't talk to the internet. If a laptop, for instance, was exploited and an access tool installed that monitored Twitter posts for tasking was taken inside a secure facility with no network connection, the tool itself would still be trying to reach out for tasking but would be unable to reach Twitter. Though this situation itself means that the perpetrating state loses the ability to communicate with that system and the access tool, it could lead to the discovery of the access tool on the system as it is continually trying to reach out to the internet from a non-internet-connected network which may be caught by defensive software or devices as being anomalous or malicious.

If the access tool was discovered due to this loss of control, it could lead to a loss of ownership. Discovering an access tool on a secure network, an enemy may perform forensics on the device and ultimately learn how to recreate the access tool for their own use. The command and control aspects of an access tool may not seem very valuable or pose a significant risk if they fall into enemy hands, but there are other portions to an access tool that might. If an access tool, for instance, had previously unknown stealth capabilities, able to get past security scans, or had new persistence mechanisms able to survive a reboot or a hard drive wipe, these would be dangerous resources if the enemy can determine how to use them. Similar to the exploit example, the enemy could also simply incorporate this new knowledge into their defensive capabilities, meaning any existing similar access tools are either discovered or nullified.

We have already discussed the concepts of environmental keying to prevent access tools from being used on systems they were not meant for or even executed for forensics analysis in a lab. Anti-tamper capabilities can delete the tool upon inspection by enemy security personnel as well. Access tools should also address the loss of control resulting from an inability to receive new tasking. A solution to this might be setting up a certain number of unsuccessful call-out attempts now resulting in the tool uninstalling itself or a similar functionality to ensure that eventually, upon loss of control, it will do its best to avoid a loss of ownership of that resource.

Attack Effects

There is the possibility that control of attack effects is lost in a similar fashion to exploits. If the tool is discovered on a system, there is a chance that even without fully understanding or reverse engineering the tool, an enemy is able to execute it against systems similar to the one it was designed for. It would be safe to say that the danger for both loss of control and ownership is higher with an attack effect that an exploit or access resource. This is because exploit and access resources are typically intended to not be noticed. Attack effects on the other hand are warfighting actions designed to have a noticeable effect on enemy systems.

Though an attack effect itself is not going to spread by itself (that would be an exploit), there is still a potential for a loss of control. As in some of the examples covered in this book, attack effects may be executed from a launch point machine against a remote one. What if that launch point machine was a virtual machine or backed up in its entirety and then deployed to other networks within the enemy state. This would result in the attack effect being launched from copies of the original launch point but in networks that were not the intended target of the attack effect. This not only poses a greater danger to a loss of ownership, but the loss of control means the perpetrating state may be responsible for acts of cyber war being inadvertently launched against non-combatants.

Losing ownership of an attack effect is also a serious concern. Having an enemy able to recreate an attack effect means it could be used against friendly systems and other third parties. Just as with exploits, publicly known and available resources can be used to carry out attack effects, including operating system commands that come installed with software like Microsoft Windows. It is not very concerning if an enemy learns that the perpetrating state used the del command to delete files in a cyber-attack. On the other hand, if the attack effect was exclusive and therefore a resource of only the perpetrating state, the enemy coming to share ownership of it is a serious loss of capability and a potential danger to wider global cyber systems.

Precautions should be taken to avoid the replay like issues of the virtualized launch point example or the recreation of tailored attack effects by an enemy to use against friendly forces and those uninvolved in the conflict. To this end, if a specialized attack effect is needed, then it should be tailored as much as possible to the specific target at hand. This way if the enemy is able to capture the capability's and recreate it, they will similarly have an extremely limited target set of potential victims. This does go against resiliency efforts at making an attack effect that is likely to be useful longer and against a wider array of targets, but if the attack effect is dangerous enough, then it is a worthwhile sacrifice to ensure it is not effectively repurposed by the enemy.

Obfuscation Infrastructure

If discovered by an enemy, the perpetrating state may lose control of its obfuscation resources with little to no effort by victim state. Denial-of-service attacks are unsophisticated but effective. If the obfuscation infrastructure is identified as being related to operational resources found in the enemy cyberspace, the enemy can simply send so much traffic at the obfuscation infrastructure that the perpetrating state can no longer communicate through it. Control can also be lost of such infrastructure if the larger networks which obfuscation and redirection systems are a part of have communication issues. If an internet service provider for the third-party network which hosts the obfuscation infrastructure is having issues, it can affect operations by the perpetrating state no longer being able to communicate with/through or control its redirection points.

Losing ownership of obfuscation infrastructure is especially dangerous to missions, conflicts, and a cyber war in general. Losing ownership of obfuscation infrastructure would happen if the enemy or another entity were able to exploit and gain privileged access to that system without the knowledge of the perpetrating state. If this happened, not only would the system no longer obfuscate the activity of the perpetrating state, but the enemy could use its new access to stealthily hamper ongoing operations, have direct knowledge of capabilities and activities, or, worse, continue attempts to swim upstream toward the perpetrating state's own frontend and backend infrastructure.

Every precaution should be taken to maintain the security of obfuscation infrastructure to avoid possible compromise by enemy hackers. This can be accomplished through both security software and standards and efforts to avoid attribution to operational resources. If the obfuscation systems are not tied to operational resources in the enemy cyberspace, then the enemy will not have reason to target them with denial or hacking attempts in the first place.

Frontend and Backend Infrastructure

Control of frontend and backend infrastructure can be lost if that infrastructure no longer affords the perpetrating state the ability to communicate to and across the internet or receive communications from other resources. This would also mean that the backend infrastructure receives no information to process and is handicapped in its further usefulness as already collected operational and intelligence data becomes increasingly dated. The loss of control and ownership both for frontend and backend systems is likely to only come if they are attributed and successfully targeted by enemy cyber warfighting activities.

Lack of functionality due to a loss of control is damaging to ongoing operations; however, enemy ownership of frontend or backend cyber systems is a damning situation. If this were to occur, it would mean the enemy is within the intelligence gathering and warfighting apparatus of the perpetrating state.

Compromise of this level is unlikely as it would involve the enemy state identifying and attributing each system in the chain of cyberspace operations from exploit or access tool all the way back to backend infrastructure. For this to be done, it would also require that attribution and system exploitation by the enemy be unknown to the perpetrating state. If the perpetrating state detects attribution of any resource, the repercussions should be determined and all mitigating steps implemented to avoid further tying of resources. For instance, if it becomes known to the perpetrating state that the enemy has identified an access tool, it would be in their best interest to immediately cull any resources related to it. Such resources might be obfuscation and redirection systems used to carry its communications back to frontend infrastructure or exploits used to install the access tool on the system. These responses should be well thought out in efforts to mitigate the impact of enemy attribution or loss of control or ownership to other resources or operations.

Tactics, Techniques, and Procedures

Regarding the loss of control and ownership, I have decided to combine the personnel-related resources of skills and tradecraft into a single resource of tactics, techniques, and procedures, or TTPs. TTPs in essence are the signature behaviors of any group whether they are a special force's unit or cyber warfighting operators or criminal hackers. Actors are often characterized and attributed by the security industry largely by their TTPs. This is how hacks and attacks are associated with one group of hackers or another or one state or another.

A state perpetrating cyber warfare actions loses control over its TTPs when they have been sufficiently attributed to identify the uniqueness of the perpetrating state. Once the enemy realizes that TTPs represent a singular entity acting against them, they can begin responding to that specific entity. This could lead to the identification of the actor behind the TTPs which would possibly lead to political and international issues. It also means that the enemy can characterize the perpetrating state's behavior and better defend themselves from it and detect it. At this level of fidelity, the enemy can also pass along these known TTPs to the security community at large or their allies which could hamper the perpetrating state's cyber operations against other targets.

Ownership of TTPs is lost when an enemy has a high enough fidelity in understanding the perpetrating state's TTPs that it can emulate them to a degree where they are indistinguishable. This poses a serious problem as the enemy can now operate under a mantle that allows them to be perceived as the perpetrating state. Such a capability could be used by the enemy to draw other states into the conflict by making it seem that the perpetrating state is also conducting cyber warfare against them. Even if the perpetrating state realizes this and changes to no longer be similar, the perception will remain, especially if at loss of control of its TTPs the perpetrating state was attributed to the public by the enemy prior to them sharing ownership of those TTPs. Short of coming out and admitting that if the actions were at first done by the perpetrating state but that it no longer operates that way, the perception would stay that it was the perpetrating state performing the activity whether it was the enemy in its guise or not.

Losing control and ownership of TTPs is clearly a slippery and dangerous slope. Avoiding this involves the constant effort to avoid attribution. More than that the perpetrating state must enforce a standard for the constant evolution and alteration of the behavior of its cyber warfighters. Not getting caught and consistently changing are the most important efforts that can be taken to ensure a state's control and ownership of its personnel-related resources.

People

The warfighters themselves may be the most valued resource we discuss, but they also present the greatest potential damage to the cyber warfighting capability of a nation if control or ownership is lost. Losing control of a cyber warfighter means that the actions of that warfighter are no longer at the direction of the perpetrating state. This can be a situation where the cyber warfighter no longer follows rules such as tradecraft or rules of engagement. Loss of control over an operator carrying out cyber warfighting actions risks compromising many other resources. If it is ever determined that a cyber warfighter is no longer acting under the control of the perpetrating state, that individual should be removed from operational status in a conflict until control can be guaranteed over that individual's actions.

Loss of ownership of a cyber warfighter is when the perpetrating state no longer has the ability to exclusively dictate the actions of that cyber warfighter. This is where insider threats become real and pose critical danger to the warfighting capabilities of a state. Ownership of a warfighter can happen when that warfighter decides to take ownership of themselves in their capacity. This situation happens when an individual, completely of their own volition, decides to perform actions of their own motivation using the state's resources. This could be something as personal as using a state-developed exploit to access an ex-lover's personal systems to get revenge. It could also be revenge against the state itself, using attack effects against friendly targets, if the individual felt slighted enough to do so. Another possibility for the loss of ownership over the cyber warfighter resource is if that individual begins to act at the direction of a foreign or enemy handler. At this point the cyber warfighter is now an agent of the other state and essentially an enemy themselves. All of these insider threat scenarios manifest themselves as loss of control or ownership of the cyber warfighting resource and in a time of war are potentially treason.

Laws themselves haven't been able to deter the loss of control or ownership of human assets whether they are cyber warfighters, infantry, FBI agents, or spies. Efforts should be made to avoid the circumstances that motivated individuals such as Aldrich Ames to feel so slighted by their own state that they act out on their own volition. The same and more must be done to avoid enemies and foreign states from gaining sufficient influence over internally developed cyber warfighters to take control and ownership of those resources.

Summary

In this chapter we covered the concepts of resource control and ownership. We discussed how the loss of each pose a threat to the warfighting capabilities of a state. Further we went over the exemplar cyber resources and how control and ownership could potentially be lost for each of them. This was done to show the extreme pace with which cyber resources can become lost or turned against the perpetrating state or third parties in a cyber war and mitigations against this were also provided.

CHAPTER 13

Challenges

Chief among the challenges faced by those wishing to conduct warfare within the cyber domain are the misconceptions that lead to ill-informed policy, planning, and execution regarding cyber activity. Misconceptions surrounding cyber warfare stem from essentially two causes. One reason for many misconceptions is a lack of technical understanding for what is actually involved in carrying out warfighting actions within the cyber domain. The other reason that cyber warfare is generally misunderstood or misrepresented is that most individuals, even in the military and government, do not adequately understand the authorities, definitions, and legality which are involved in warfare in general and specifically how they apply to the cyber domain of warfighting.

To truly appreciate how technology constrains cyber warfighting activity involves at least notional understanding of a wide spectrum of cyber technologies. As such, even those cyber professionals technically proficient in one aspect or another of the resources needed to carry out cyber warfare may not fully comprehend the abundance and diversity of technical challenges. It is easy to focus on the cyber tools and technology involved in exploitation and attack effects because those are what are readily associated with cyber warfare. As we have laid out through the chapters in this book, the technical challenges also involve a diverse infrastructure and skill requirement to successfully carry out cyber operations from friendly cyberspace, across the internet, and into target enemy systems.

Even those individuals who readily understand Title 10 and Title 50 of the US Code and how they provide authorization and oversight to cyber warfighting actions need further comprehension of cyber. We have discussed many examples of how certain cyber actions when viewed through the frame of those titles actually represent potential war crimes or illegal actions. We must ensure that an understanding of cyber warfare is not limited to what lets us conduct war within the cyber domain but includes the information required to keep such actions just and within lines of international convention as well.

© Jacob G. Oakley 2019
J. G. Oakley, *Waging Cyber War*, https://doi.org/10.1007/978-1-4842-4950-5_13

Having policy makers and commanders involved in cyber warfare with offensive security backgrounds would make them potentially better positioned to make informed and legal cyber warfighting decisions. This is obviously a solution that isn't going to manifest itself, but it represents the type of background that would provide operational insight into cyber warfare just as it has for me. Combining such knowledge with military or government experience would be the ideal genesis for creating the cyber combatant commanders and house and senate armed services oversight committees of the future, prepared to handle this new domain of warfare. More realistically, as citizens who grew up with computers and access to the internet become senior leaders, military commanders, and politicians, there will at least be a much higher baseline computer and internet knowledge among those groups which will naturally lead to decisions and commands that better reflect and leverage this cyber understanding.

In the same way, I think the legality and authority issues of cyber warfare will become more easily understood with time, as will strategy and tactics regarding cyber warfare. Once you have leaders and warfighters who have grown up with cyber warfare and cyber domain activities existing and being carried out, strategy will better employ it. Imagine the advent of airplanes in warfare. At the time, there were no senior commanders, generals, or government leaders who had gone through their lives with an understanding of airplanes and their military applications. As such, you have people attempting to execute strategic planning and tactical decisions with the addition of a warfighting implement they potentially do not understand and assuredly are not accustomed to. The same is the case for the cyber domain, as it continues to influence and be connected to other domains of warfare, it will be better understood, leveraged, and executed.

Major Misconceptions

Resulting from the knowledge gaps in technology and legality are the major misconceptions which challenge the successful implementation of the cyber domain as an adequate and appropriate warfighting environment. The following are not representative of the totality of challenges faced in conducting cyber warfare and cyber activities, but in my opinion, they are some of the most impactful.

Exploitation Is Warfare

Cyber exploitation and intelligence gathering activities by foreign adversaries are continually referred to as cyber-attacks. This use of vernacular permeates from the media into the minds of those who ingest it. For this and other reasons, cyber activities which are not attack effects or battlefield preparation are constantly referred to as attacks or cyber warfare. We have established that this is incorrect. Title 50 activities are not acts of war whether they are committed by the United States or other nations and we need to remember that.

When a foreign spy is discovered in the United States, they are not shot; they are tried, convicted, and incarcerated or depending on their political or diplomatic status simply expelled. The US government itself has taken this same stance with cyber actors in its charging through the Department of Justice and Federal Bureau of Investigations of attributed uniformed hackers from China and other countries. This should further enforce the fact that for a cyber activity to fall within the legal and authoritative realm of warfare, it must actually be a fully attributed state-sponsored attack effect.

Even when conducted by uniformed members of a foreign country as part of state-sponsored cyber intelligence gathering, it is considered intelligence gathering under Title 10–type authorities and not Title 10 warfighting actions and authorities. As such, it would be outside the authorities of most national and certainly international convention for a state to respond to such exploitation or intelligence gathering activities with their own cyber-attack effects. This would certainly be viewed as an unprovoked warfighting action and potentially a declaration of open conflict.

Ease of Attribution

There is not a widespread appreciation for the sheer difficulty in attributing cyber activity. This is the case for exploitation, intelligence gathering, and attack effects launched within the cyber domain. Especially where cyber-attack effects, which are acts of war, attribution must be with absolute fidelity if a response is to be launched. We need to remember that a response to an act of cyber warfare can be a missile launch, invasion, or otherwise similarly weaponized warfighting action. Since that is the case and given the ease with which cyber actions can be masked and attribution undermined, convincing decision makers and politicians to declare war or approve warfighting activity based on an attribution of a cyber-attack effect would seem extremely unlikely.

There are essentially two ways in which a cyber-attack effect can elicit a warfighting response within a realistic time window. The state which launched the cyber warfighting action can openly admit the act as part of a declaration of hostilities against its enemy. The only other situation that responsibly allows for warfighting responses to a cyber-attack effect is when the attributed perpetrator is a state with which the victim and responding state is already in open conflict. These two scenarios revolve around open acknowledgment of motivation for the cyber-attack. Short of the perpetrator admitting it was a Title 10–type action, in cyber, there is essentially no way to know the intent of a cyber activity without it resulting in an attack effect or being admitted as an effort to bring one to bear. When part of a declaration of hostilities or ongoing conflict, motivation is admitted or assumed.

Return Fire

In cyber warfare there is no realistic concept of return fire. If we ignore the previous misconception and assume attribution is actually possible, there is still no feasible situation where it would happen so fast that cyber or other actions could subsequently be launched against the unit or asset which launched the attack effect. Remember, a tool which delivers an attack effect can be installed days, months, or even years prior to being executed. Further, even if the enemy hackers are discovered placing the attack tool, without execution having happened, there is no way to completely know, or more importantly prove, the motivation of that action. When the necessity for timeliness is combined with the near impossibility of attribution in the first place, return fire seems a laughable concept. Cyber-attack effects should be directed as a strategic decision as part of a greater and wider conflict, not as part of a tactical response to an ongoing firefight.

I like to compare the ridiculous concept of returning fire in the cyber domain to the following example. Imagine US patrol in Afghanistan accidently came across a Soviet-era land mine, placed decades earlier to deter afghan advances. The land mine is stepped on by one of the patrol members and it explodes. The mine was placed by Soviet soldiers who are potentially dead of old age and are certainly no longer even in the country of Afghanistan. What target might the surviving members of the patrol return fire against? This may seem like an exaggeration, but it would be just as easy for the members of that patrol to go back in time and return fire against the Soviet soldiers who placed the mines as it would for a victim of a cyber-attack effect to attribute, target, and respond in a tactical manner to the assets which launched the cyber-attack with their own cyber-attack capabilities.

Target Dictation

There is this idea that once targets are found in the cyber domain, commanders can simply direct them be attacked and it will be so. What makes the return fire scenario even more improbable is the fact that target dictation in the cyber domain happens as the result of vulnerabilities being present and weaponized exploits existing. Commanders and decision makers cannot dictate which targets are susceptible or which capabilities exist. So even in a scenario where we ignore that attribution is extremely difficult and successfully targeting for return fire next to impossible, we may still be unable to respond to that target with cyber-attack effects. Let's assume attribution was essentially immediate and with enough fidelity to responsibly dictate a response against the enemy who conducted it. We must also assume that the enemy that conducted it has not simply been attributed but that the location from which it is obfuscating its communication pathways or accessing the internet to conduct cyber operations has also been located and with enough fidelity to adequately target it. For return fire to happen while the aggressors are still carrying out cyber-attack effects would also mean that the infrastructure identified as being actively used by the enemy is vulnerable to an exploit in the arsenal of the responding state and that an attack effect that is viable on the enemy device is available.

Resource Availability

In case we have not yet decided that cyber warfare is insanely difficult or potentially wholly unrealistic, there is more! In the same line as the misconception that targets in the cyber domain can simply be chosen based on a decision by a commander is the incorrect assumption that tools are readily available. I don't just mean the exploit and attack tools, but also the ability to even communicate with a target once it is chosen or operate interactively on that target with an access tool if it can be exploited.

The difficulty in attaining the technological resources involved in cyber warfare coupled with the potential ease with which control or ownership may be lost would have to weigh so heavily on every warfighting decision it might paralyze the cyber operator and the commander alike. Let's do some more assuming to continue illustrating the difficulty in cyber warfare these misconceptions help decision makers ignore. Let's assume a cyber-attack effect was launched, and the victim not only attributed the perpetrator but identified the infrastructure they were actively using to launch more cyber-attack effects against other assets of the victim state. The commander picks that infrastructure as a target and cyber-attack effects as the appropriate response action. Let's even assume the victim state has both a working exploit against those systems and an attack effect that will nullify the enemy's cyber warfighting capability. The decision that is now faced by the commander is, is it worth it? Remember, using an exploit and/or an attack effect potentially risks the loss of control or ownership of that resource.

Imagine a patrol in enemy territory is engaged by enemy small arms fire. Now imagine that the patrol leader has to weigh the fact that if he or she responds in kind with small arms fire from their M-16 assault rifles, there is a chance that the M-16 weapon as a resource might be lost, not to the patrol, but to the entire state military. This is an unrealistic situation in the domain of land warfare, but in the cyber domain, it is very real, and assuming all other challenges leading to an ability to return fire or engage an enemy with cyber-attack effects were satisfactorily accomplished, there is still the question of whether or not the risk to the cyber resource itself is worth it in the given scenario. Would you be willing to risk an exploit and attack effect resource in a cyber return fire response against enemy cyber infrastructure if that same exploit and attack effect would be needed to shut down enemy air warning radar ahead of troop deployments and air strikes? I don't think I would. This is further in support of the fact that cyber domain warfighting activity should be strategically planned and weighed at the theater or global level and not a part of tactical responses in ongoing battles as the potential implications of cyber resource utilization are so far-reaching.

Shelf Life

There are resource assumptions beyond the misconceptions about the general availability of cyber resources both in general and in a target-specific sense. There is a notional concept that these resources can be stockpiled and kept of the shelf so that when the time comes for use, the potential for their loss is less damaging to the overall cyber warfighting capability. The fact is that this is simply not the case. Even if a state had the ability to create stockpiles of different exploits, access tools, and attack effects, there is no guarantee that when the time comes that they are utilized, they are effective. There is an entire global industry sector dedicated to securing cyber systems from being subject to exploitation, unauthorized access, and attack.

An attack effect or exploit may still work and the vulnerability enabling their execution on the target may still be present, but the security industry may have developed signatures based on similar capabilities already seen or simply improve heuristics to the point that they detect the tools as malicious and stop them. Cyber security companies don't care if a tool is an amateur hacker backdoor or a state created zero-day exploit. They are doing their best every day to stop all types and sources of potentially malicious cyber activity. This means that even if the ability to stockpile cyber resources were realistic, stockpiling them in the first place may be a wasteful endeavor. Aside from the security industry, there are also any number of other states, organized crime entities, and hacker groups trying to also develop cyber resources, which may be almost identical to what is stockpiled. These facts also further complicate that decision paralysis on whether or not to risk losing a cyber resource through its utilization as it may be lost at any time even if never utilized.

Static Targets

Just as there is a misconception that once developed, a cyber resource is readily available to be used until needed, there is an assumption that targets are static. I mean static in two ways. The first assumption is that once a resource is developed for use against a target, that target will remain in a state which allows for the cyber resource to function. The second assumption is that the target's location will remain the same in the time between target determination and response execution.

Every key stroke, second of being powered on, and on off flip of a bit changes the state of a cyber system which makes them extremely volatile targets. Pretend every earlier misconception were true and a target has been attributed as enemy cyber infrastructure and exploits and attack effects exist for it and the decision has been made to use those tools against it and no security industry development challenges the tool's execution. In the time it took to do all of this, the enemy may have moved infrastructure, or more likely left the system up, which was never theirs to begin with, and moved their tools and operation elsewhere on the internet. In this case the cyber-attack response by the victim may actually be taking place against a system owned by a non-combatant. If this system were grandma's smart fridge, no big deal, if it was a machine in a hospital used to track medication dosages and allergies, we suddenly have a potential war crime and innocent casualties on our hands.

The previous scenario illustrates the challenge with the speed of target location change in the cyber domain. To show dynamic the state of cyber system targets, imagine the enemy systems were all using the Microsoft Windows 7 operating system and had been prepared several months ahead of time for a widespread attack to cut off power to military and government forces ahead of an invasion. Now, in those months Microsoft announced and implemented an automatic update of all Windows 7 and newer systems to the Windows 10 operating system. Now the targets with cyber-attack tools on them are no longer vulnerable to the attack effect or its executing exploit.

Next Hacker Up

In the Marines and many other military organizations especially, there is the concept of next man or woman up. If one Marine or soldier goes down or cannot perform their duty, there is an entire Marine Corps or Army full of troops ready and willing to take their place. While this is a stoic concept and useful in some settings, it is not a realistic scenario in the cyber domain of warfighting. I have heard with my own ears a senior leader say to highly trained and specialized cyber operators, "you are not special, I can replace you with any Marine." While I appreciate the intent of warfighters not thinking they are better or special or deserving of accolades and special treatment over those in other military occupational fields, it is ignorant of certain facts. You can't just replace a pilot, medical doctor, or special forces soldier with anyone from the larger forces. Cyber warfighters should be no different. The time it takes to develop the type of skills red teamers and penetration testers have which is needed to conduct cyber operations takes years and at least a commiserate level of knowledge if not formal education in computer science at the post-graduate level. The military and government services often struggle with this as they are organizations that rely on an ability to replace individuals, whether due to promotion, duty location rotation, or change in responsibilities. As such, cyber warfighters must be viewed as an extremely limited resource, especially given the ease with which they could find themselves employed outside of the military or federal service.

Open Conflict

Most of this book has covered the technological and conceptual challenges to war within the cyber domain as seen in a vacuum. While all true and applicable out of a vacuum, they do not capture the greatest potential challenge to using cyber as a warfighting domain. In an open conflict with another nation, such as another state or states, like happened in the World Wars, the cyber domain may not be available. There is a potential that the enemy has completely shut itself off from cyber communications with the rest of the world, making cyber warfare almost entirely ineffective. There is also the potential in a wide enough conflict that the cyber domain ceases to exist altogether. Imagine World War III, GPS and communication satellites are shot out of space with missiles, undersea cables are cut, nuclear weapons and EMPs are detonated. In such a scenario, pooling resources into cyber warfare seems foolhardy. I am not suggesting that the cyber domain and cyber operations aren't extremely important, and still worth pursuit in an open conflict situation, but using what little access might be obtained in such a conflict is likely to be far more important as an intelligence gathering mechanism than a conduit for a one-time cyber-attack effect.

Open Conflict Challenges

Supposing in an open conflict the infrastructure which enables the cyber domain was not specifically targeted with kinetic weaponry, there are still specific challenges to leveraging cyber-attack effects in times of open war, and in many cases cyber-attack effects are inferior for one or all of the following reasons to more conventional warfighting options commanders may have at their disposal.

Target Availability

As already discussed, targets have to present an attack surface reachable via the cyber domain to be part and parcel to cyber warfare. Even if attacks are not directed at systems which enable this attack surface to be reached between states across the cyber domain, incidental damage from conventional warfare in the same conflict may similarly limit the ability to reach cyber systems with attack effects. More than that, enemies are likely to go into states of self-seclusion particularly in the cyber domain knowing that maintaining an internet or otherwise interconnected presence for cyber systems poses an elevated risk.

Communication Dependability

The timing of cyber-attack effects is very important as many times such tools are used in concert with other operations during a conflict. As such, these tools are likely deployed ahead of the operations they support and are expected to be executed at the appropriate time. For much the same reasons the attack surface may not be available in the first place, communication lines between the perpetrating state and its cyber-attack effects can be easily lost due to incidental damage from kinetic strikes, if those systems aren't already the target themselves of kinetic weapons. There are potential mitigations for this in having triggered attack effects and other automatic execution mechanisms, but if the system loses power around the time the attack is needed or the system acting as a launch point is otherwise effected, attack effect execution and communication with access and other tools can be undependable.

Ineffective Weaponry

Assuming targets can be reached and are available for the deployment of cyber-attack effects, there is the possibility that the target for one reason or another has become resilient or resistant to the cyber exploitation or attack effect. We have covered many reasons why this may be the case, regardless of why having a warfighting domain with weapons which have elevated chances of becoming ineffective is a dangerous asset to rely on as part of a wider warfighting repertoire. This could be exceedingly frustrating to commanders and decision makers as the various assets in the cyber arsenal may not reveal themselves as ineffective until the moment they are relied upon and executed.

No Battle Damage Assessment

Another important concept for a warfighting domain as part of a greater open conflict is the ability for commanders and warfighters to recognize the effectiveness of their strikes. This helps steer the commander toward continued or altering utilization of various weapon systems and warfighting resources. If you shoot ten missiles at an enemy aircraft and all of them miss or cause negligible damage, you may switch weapon systems used to engage such aircraft in the ongoing firefight and in future skirmishes. With cyber-attack effects, there is a difficulty in determining the battle damage assessment and overall effectiveness. This is the case in a vacuum where the attack effects themselves are likely responsible for a lack of communication with the target once executed, the situation is exacerbated in open conflict where any of the previously discussed communication impacts or issues could also lead to a difficulty in observing effects on a cyber system after it has been attacked via the cyber domain. Without knowing whether or not a valuable cyber exploit or attack is effective, a commander may suffer further still decision paralysis with continued use. Is it worth more deployments of a valuable exploit and attack effect that may be better used for more important targets down the road if you cannot determine its effectiveness against current targets? Probably not.

Cost-Effectiveness

Access to enemy cyber systems, especially in an open conflict, is an extremely valuable source of information. In an open conflict, the entire conventional arsenal is available to a commander in most cases. Choosing to give up or endanger an intelligence gathering source such as a cyber system, where a cheap and easy to re-produce missile can also accomplish similar strategic effects, comes across as irresponsible. In a conflict where enemies are already engaged in open conventional warfare with bombs, missiles, bullets, and artillery, justifying using a cyber-attack effect in their stead is hard to picture. I am not saying scenarios wouldn't exist where cyber-attack effects might not be the best option. However, in open conflict, the cost-benefit of using and risking cyber resources like exploits and access tools to launch attack effects within the cyber domain is hard to justify.

Summary

In this chapter we covered the major misconceptions surrounding the concept of cyber warfare. We also discussed some of the cultural and environmental issues that lead to these misconceptions that are both generational and technical in nature. Next we discussed the concept of open conflict and how it affects aspects of cyber warfare, including the existence of the cyber warfighting domain itself. The challenges to cyber warfare in an open conflict were also covered.

CHAPTER 14

Contemplation

This book has hopefully been a journey to a deeper understanding of cyber warfare, what it actually means, and what the real technical and non-technical challenges would be faced in the process of carrying out warfighting actions in the cyber domain. Now that we know how it really works, I think it is worth exploring the question of, should it work?

The cyber domain and both Title 10– and Title 50–type activities within it are extremely powerful tools to add to a state's defensive apparatus and offensive arsenal. It is my belief that these resources should primarily be utilized and strategized as the unconventional capability they represent. When there is not open conflict, the intelligence gathering and covert action capabilities made available through the cyber domain cannot be ignored. However, it is in my opinion that trying to force the cyber domain as a warfighting resource in open conflict and alongside conventional warfare is not necessarily responsible.

There certainly are potential scenarios for the effective use of cyber warfare, but its true strategic value will likely not be realized until commanders and decision makers and warfighters alike come to a sufficient understanding of how cyber affects warfare and how war works in the cyber domain. Even presented with all of the information in this book, there may be individuals who still want to fire cyber bullets at the enemy; for those individuals and for any of you who read this book but want a quicker way to convey to others why cyber warfare doesn't work the way they think, I have a useful analogy you can make.

Biological Warfare

Let's focus for a minute on a concept most people will readily agree with. Biological warfare is a terribly irresponsible and ineffective way to wage war. National and international laws forbid its use. The Geneva Convention and other international bodies and agreements disparage it, and even before the world wised up and agreed to stand against biological warfare, it was extremely ineffective. Let's take some time to cover why this is.

Communicability

Biological agents are dangerous because they can spread from individual to individual making a small deployment have effects against a large target set. Unfortunately, biological agents don't necessarily spread with any reliability. This means that a commander could launch a biological attack with a target in mind, but that deployment of biological agents may not end up spreading to anywhere near the number of targets necessary to achieve the strategic goal of deploying it.

Effectiveness

Even if successfully deployed and spreading to 100% of the intended target set, biological agents do not have a guaranteed mortality rate of 100%. So, even if all enemy combatants are infected with a biological agent, there is going to be some percentage of them that make it through the infection and are still able to fight. There is also the fact that biological agents affect people at different speeds, so even if say 60% of those infected ended up dying, they may not be dead for weeks and that presents an undeterminable timetable for biological weapons. This means that if a commander were to use biological agents, they would have to plan their strategies around the fact that when they deploy a biological weapon against a target, there is no way of knowing how effective it will ultimately be.

Targetability

Probably the scariest aspect of biological warfare is the inability to guarantee with any kind of certainty that a biological agent will only affect those it was intended to target. Biological weapons may be launched against an enemy troop garrison, but a change in wind direction could blow the biological agent to a nearby town. Environmental changes aside, the fact that biological agents are indiscriminately communicable means that as troops take time off, visit their families, or are otherwise around non-combatants, including medical and supply staff, they can be spreading the weaponized agent to those non-combatants.

No Battle Damage Assessment

Given that once launched, a biological agent will take an unknown amount of time to spread to an unknown amount of targets who will themselves feel the effects of that agent at an unknown rate, and incubation time means commanders have almost no way of knowing how effective use of a biological agent may have been. Further, conducting battle damage assessment is unsafe. This is both because of the agent itself and because of the fact that there is no way of knowing if it successfully achieved the strategic goal of neutralizing enemy forces. If it was less effective than expected or had a longer incubation period against the targets than thought, they would potentially still be there ready to fight.

Control

Morality and ethical issues aside, the potential for a biological agent to quickly spread out of control means a single deployment could be devastating far beyond the commander's intent. What if a biological agent, instead of taking longer to spread or have noticeable results, was on the other end of the spectrum? What if the agent spread far more effectively than was expected, infecting innocents and non-combatants and enemy troops alike? What if it became a pandemic and ended up causing devastating losses indiscriminately across the globe? The problem is there is no way to have a biological agent with an effective off switch.

Ownership

Ignoring the moral dilemmas and the lack of control or targetability and other strategic and tactical issues with biological warfare there is the aspect of ownership which makes it an ineffective weapon. Once a biological agent is deployed, the enemy can begin analyzing it as can third parties. There is a distinct possibility the enemy can take the biological agent and make it more effective, turning it back on the perpetrating state. There is also the potential that upon using the biological agent once, the enemy and other third parties are able to create a vaccine for it. Therefore, all the dangerous work that went into creating the weapon could be undone after one deployment making it a potentially target and use specific resource which is not ideal for warfighting. Further, through natural medical research efforts, strains similar to the biological agent may be found and vaccines created even while the biological weapon was waiting on the shelf to be used. There are also many mitigating capabilities to such weapons such as gas masks and other protective gear made for toxic environments.

Bringing It Together

I am in no way suggesting that cyber warfare should be internationally disavowed and never utilized because it is like biological warfare. The issues of cruelty and inhumane pain and suffering that come with biological agents have more to do with it being banned than do its tactical and strategic shortcomings. Now, if you were to ask someone strategically why using biological warfare as part of a greater conflict wouldn't make sense and you followed up with some of the reasons just discussed, you would probably get nods of agreement. These biological warfare-related reasons are very similar to some of the reasons why large-scale warfare within the cyber domain won't work as an effective tactical or strategic resource.

In open conflict the communications paths needed to carry out cyber warfighting are susceptible to interruption just as communicability in the use of biological agents cannot guarantee it spreads to the intended targets. Cyber exploits or attack effects and biological agents suffer from the same issues with effectiveness where there is no guarantee that the target needing a desired end effect will be vulnerable to the facilitating mechanism. Target troops can be resistant or less affected by biological agents than anticipated, and cyber targets may be invulnerable to the cyber resources in the perpetrating state's arsenal.

Though to a lesser extent than biological warfare, cyber tools, especially those that rely on self-propagation such as worms, create targetability concerns. Both types of warfare have infectious weapons which cannot guarantee with adequate certainty that they will not spread to non-combatants and third parties not involved in conflict. Both also have the same volatile attributes that mean assessing their effectiveness post deployment can be next to impossible.

There is also the risks to ownership both types of warfare share. Huge investments are involved in developing weaponized cyber exploits and attack effects as well as biological agents. Ignoring the moral dilemma of using biological weapons, there is a serious concern for the cost-benefit of using it in formal widespread warfare just as there is with cyber tools. These resources risk becoming understood, copied, and reapplied by enemies and third parties alike. Further, there are the risks that those resources become nullified by natural developments of the medical or cyber security industries.

Summary

In this chapter we discussed biological warfare and without consideration for its ethical failings, that it falls short of a strategically deployable and tactically dependable weapon and form of warfare. This more widely understood concept was used as an analogy to more easily explain some of the reasons cyber warfare does not factually work as a standard domain of warfare as it is often misunderstood to be. The analogy is not perfect but hopefully leads to a more tempered understanding and approaches to deploying cyber warfighting resources in congruence with conventional conflicts.

Index

A

Access tools, 84
    local privilege, 103
    local unprivileged, 102
    non-local privileged, 103
    non-local unprivileged, 103
    target relationship
        access noticed, 106–108
        access unnoticed, 109–112
        DoS, 106
        ICBM, 106
    types
        interactive access, 105
        none, 104
        non-interactive access, 104
Anti-aircraft capabilities, 53
Association
    incidental, 134, 135
    package/packet traversal, 134
    purposeful
        to distract, 139
        obfuscation, 136–138
        self-attribution, 140
        weapon, 140, 141
    tracert, 132–134

B

Battle damage assessment (BDA), 94, 95, 151
Biological warfare

battle damage assessment, 183
communicability, 182
control, 183
definition, 181
effectiveness, 182
ownership, 183
target, 182
tools, 184

C

Central Intelligence Agency (CIA), 13, 14, 17, 107
Communications intelligence (COMINT), 57
Cyber access operations, 112, 113
Cyber-attack
    espionage, 54, 55
    noise level, 41, 42
    relationship, 44, 45
    Title 10, 42–44
    types
        deny, enemy (*see* Enemy denying)
        manipulation, enemy (*see* Enemy manipulating)
    warfighting, 45
Cyber domain collection
    direct collection, 66, 67
    human source
        cyber reconnaissance, 65
        espionage, 64

© Jacob G. Oakley 2019
J. G. Oakley, *Waging Cyber War*, https://doi.org/10.1007/978-1-4842-4950-5

F

G

H

I

J, K